the High Performance Cookbook

the High Performance Cookbook

150 Recipes for Peak Performance

Susan M. Kleiner Ph.D., R.D.

and **KarenRae Friedman-Kester** M.S., R.D.

Macmillan • USA

MACMILLAN
A Simon & Schuster Macmillan Company
15 Columbus Circle
New York, NY 10023

MACMILLAN is a registered trademark of
Macmillan, Inc.

Library of Congress Cataloging-in-Publication
Data
Kleiner, Susan M.
    The high performance cookbook / Susan M.
Kleiner and KarenRae Friedman-Kester.
        p.   cm.
    Includes index
    ISBN: 0-02-860370-2
    1.   Athletes—Nutrition.   2.   Cookery.
3.   Low-fat diet—Recipes.
I.   Friedman-Kester, KarenRae.   II.   Title.
TX361.A8K58   1995
94-36810   CIP
641.5'63'088796—dc20

Manufactured in the United States of America
10 9 8 7 6 5 4 3 2 1

CONTENTS

To Jeff, in pursuit of excellence.

—SMK

To know where you have come from guides you in where you are going.
To my past, present, and future: my grandparents, parents, husband, and
daughter.

—KRFK

ACKNOWLEDGMENTS

We are sincerely grateful to all the people who helped us create this book. To Justin Schwartz, our editor at Macmillan—thank you for your vision and guidance; this is your baby, too. To Maria Massey, our production editor—thanks for the polish. To Chris Alba at *Men's Fitness* magazine—thank you for publishing the article that led to the book. Many thanks to Dan Benardot for providing your Nourish Check Athlete software used for recipe analyses, and to Louis Baylog for integrating our software into a useful system. A special thank you to Grace Petot for introducing us in Food Science lab more than a few years ago.

We were so fortunate to have great people with great taste testing our recipes, providing a few, and offering a sounding board for our ideas and frustrations. Numerous thanks to Stephen Douglass, Elaine Friedman, Lee and David Goodman, Irene Kanter, Jeff Kanter, Leah and Allen Kester, Mark Kester, Randi and Eric Kester, Elinor and Ike Kleiner, Judy Schuster and Chuck Kleiner, Rochelle and Steven Walk for your innovative recipe ideas and constant attention to detail. Kudos to Mark Kester for creatively spicing the introductions to each recipe.

Finally, to all those trying to achieve peak performance—thank you for your eagerness to work hard and your drive to excel. Your passion has been our guiding light.

—SMK
KRFK

PREFACE

You wake at the crack of dawn and your mind is already at work planning your day's strategies. Whether you are heading for a sales meeting or the starting line, you're ready to face the competition. In order to perform at peak levels, eating well must be part of your strategy. If food is not in your game plan then you're sure to fatigue before you reach your goal.

Without the proper information to help you plan your high-performance diet you may have thought that eating well is just not possible for you. *The High Performance Cookbook* will give you all the information you'll need to design your own personalized diet plan, and change your attitude about eating and cooking forever.

I live your lifestyle, and I know. Many of my nutrition strategies were developed during the years that I combined a life of modern dance, graduate school, work, and performing on stage as a magician's assistant until the wee hours. As a student of nutrition, I knew that I had to eat well to succeed. And I did.

Today my life is still hectic, but in a different way. I must perform at peak levels for my work, my family, and myself. My nutrition strategy combines state of the art nutrition science with the practical needs of a high-performance lifestyle. These are the strategies and recipes that I now give to my clients, and that I use myself. The first chapter will help you decide what and how much you need to eat to achieve peak performance. Use the second chapter as a basic cooking primer. It will give you lists of the foods and utensils you should stock in your kitchen to prepare most of the recipes without a special trip to the store, as well as some basic cooking techniques for the novice cook. The recipes are designed to meet the needs of your high-performance life. They are simple to prepare yet packed with the nutrition you need to fuel your body at home, on the job, on the road, or before a race.

You can eat great food, lead a busy life, beat the competition, and stay healthy. It takes an attitude adjustment and the right information. This book will give you both.

—Dr. Susan M. Kleiner

When I think back to my first involvement with food, I see visions of homemade noodles drying on a tablecloth-covered bed or fresh baked bread cooling on the pantry. I see lemon meringue pies that were eight inches high and apple rolls that would melt in your mouth. No, I wasn't born in the last century, but both my grandmothers were. I was reared on using the finest, freshest ingredients, a vegetable garden in the backyard, and recipes you learned by feel, rather than by writing them down. The recipes were wholesome, without additives, and usually loaded with fat.

The strong cooking skills of my grandmothers was tempered with my mother's more modern belief in making it easy and a less liberal use of fat. This combination gave me the skills and confidence to mix both fresh and convenience foods in the same recipe, lower the fat on many traditional recipes and even tackle a cookbook.

In college, my love of cooking was teamed with the science of nutrition. By joining forces with Susan, my background in foods and nutrition is augmented with Susan's knowledge for a book that is grounded in the science of high-performance nutrition, yet allows for nouvelle cuisine. Favorite recipes from my childhood have been altered to meet high-performance standards.

The premise of this book is based on the idea that healthy eating can taste good and be convenient. As you utilize our recipes for achieving peak performance I hope that you achieve what you set out to do, enjoy good health, and good food.

—KarenRae Friedman-Kester

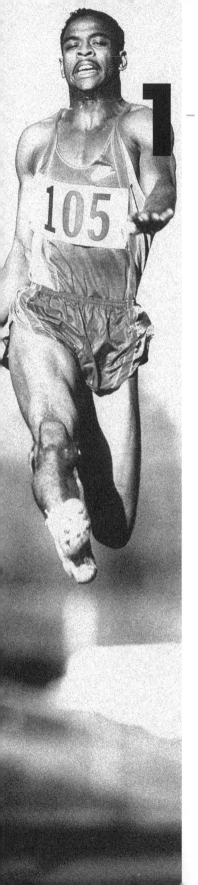

1

the HIGH-Performance Diet

THE SCIENCE OF HIGH-PERFORMANCE NUTRITION

Nutrition scientists are rapidly changing the face of the American diet and ridding us of many of the false beliefs of the past. We grew up believing that the way to stay thin was to eat a very low-calorie diet. Even more important than cutting calories was limiting starchy foods like bread, pasta, and potatoes. We were told we shouldn't drink any fluids during exercise because it would give us stomach cramps, and that the best prevention for dehydration was to take a salt tablet.

Now we know that the nutritional key to having unlimited energy is to eat plenty of food and to make most of it starchy, high-carbohydrate foods like bread, pasta, and potatoes. The more food you eat, the more vitamins and minerals you can get into your body and the healthier you will be. We know that drinking before, during, and after exercise is essential for maintaining adequate fluid balance, and that salt tablets can actually cause dehydration by pulling the water out of your intestinal cells and into your gut by osmotic pressure.

Sports nutrition recommendations are now firmly based on hard scientific evidence. Although there is still no magic bullet for gaining the competitive edge, there are definitely some important diet strategies that will help you achieve your personal best.

THE HIGH PERFORMANCE COOKBOOK

Regardless of how much you know about nutrition, you probably still have trouble planning and preparing the foods that you know you should be eating. There just doesn't seem to be enough time in the day to eat, sleep, train, work, and shop. The introductory chapters of this book will teach you how to scientifically plan your high-performance diet. Then use the delicious recipes to efficiently plan your meals, whether you are in training for competition or trying to stay in shape.

Most of the recipes take only thirty minutes to prepare, and all of them take less than an hour. They are low in fat and high in carbohydrates to meet the demands of your intense lifestyle. Each recipe is accompanied by a description of its outstanding nutrient characteristics to help you plan your menus to meet your personal nutrition needs.

Everyone has different energy needs, but most active people fall within two categories. Men are generally larger than women and have higher energy needs. To assist with portion control in the entrées' sections, we have offered two different serving sizes to meet the needs of a higher- and a lower-calorie diet. For a diet close to 3,000 calories a day, use each recipe to yield two servings. If you are extremely active and need much more than 3,000 calories a day, you might choose to eat a double serving of some of the foods. For a diet that is closer to 2,000 calories a day, get three servings out of each recipe.

CARBOHYDRATES: THE HIGH-PERFORMANCE FUEL

The most powerful nutritional factor that effects how much energy you have is the amount of carbohydrate in your diet. Research with trained subjects doing the same cycling exercise on different carbohydrate diets has shown that a high-carbohydrate diet increases endurance. On a diet that had only 25 percent of its calories as carbohydrate, it took just 90 minutes to exhaust the subjects. When they were fed 50 percent of their calories as carbohydrate, they increased their exercise time to 2 hours and 6 minutes. When the diet was increased to 75 percent carbohydrate calories, the subjects could cycle 3 hours and 9 minutes before they became exhausted. The increased endurance was attributed to an increase in the level of muscle glycogen, a form of carbohydrate stored in one's muscles after a meal high in carbohydrate has been consumed. Further research has shown that a diet made up of 65 percent carbohydrate is adequate to maintain full stores of glycogen in the muscles on a daily basis.

Why is glycogen so important? During the first few minutes of exercise your muscles are predominantly dependent on glycogen for the production of energy. Very little fat is burned as fuel at the start of exercise, because in order to burn fat there must be oxygen available. Within those first two to three minutes there hasn't been enough time to complete the metabolic processes that move oxygen into the cells that will metabolize fat into energy.

As exercise continues and oxygen is transported into the cells, fat becomes the predominant energy source and carbohydrate use drops off. After 10 minutes at maximum exercise capacity, 85 percent of the fuel used is fat and only 15 percent is carbohydrate. After 60 minutes, 98 percent of your fuel usage is from fat. The determining factor is the duration of exercise. If you can exercise at 50 percent to 60 percent of your maximum heart rate, you can exercise for a longer duration and burn more fat as fuel.

Once you begin to tire less oxygen is available to the cells. Now your muscles must return to the use of stored glycogen for your final minutes of exercise before you are completely exhausted. This is the critical point. The more glycogen that you have stored in your muscles, the more endurance you will have at the end of exercise.

Each time you exercise you use up some of your stored glycogen. It is absolutely necessary to replenish your stores by eating a 65 percent carbohydrate diet every day. In fact, it is best to eat a high-carbohydrate snack or meal containing 100 grams of carbohydrate within the first fifteen minutes to two hours after exercise. This is when your muscles will most rapidly replace the spent glycogen.

If 65 percent is good, why not eat 75 percent of your calories as carbohydrate? Because there is a general ceiling on the amount of glycogen your muscles can hold. You can fool the cells and boost that level by following a "carbohydrate-loading" regimen. But if you do this too frequently, your body will not cooperate and you will fail to gain any benefit from carbohydrate-loading. Wait at least two weeks between carbohydrate-loading regimens, and don't load more than four to six times per year. If you are in more competitions than this, just maintain a 65 percent to 75 percent carbohydrate diet during your racing season. This plan will make an obvious difference only if you are involved in an endurance activity that lasts longer than an hour.

Before an important endurance competition, you can load glycogen into your muscles by following this plan:

A. Three days prior to the event, taper your exercise to begin to rest your muscles, and boost your carbohydrate intake to 75 percent of your calorie intake but no more than 800 grams of carbohydrate a day (1 gram of carbohydrate = 4 calories). If you eat a very high-calorie diet and 65 percent is already 800 grams of carbohydrate, increase your carbohydrate intake by 10 percent.

B. The day before the competition should be a rest day, but continue to consume the high-carbohydrate diet.

What you eat for your precompetition meal, and what you drink just before and during exercise, can also affect your glycogen stores. Your precompetition meal should be eaten two to three hours beforehand and should contain 100 grams of carbohydrate. My clients who have early-morning race starts wake at 3 or 4 A.M., eat breakfast, then go back to sleep until they have to wake for the race (SMK). If you are involved in a long-distance event, drinking a sports drink with some carbohydrate in it before and during exercise will help maintain your blood sugar levels and give you an energy boost at the end of exercise.

In addition to the great energy boost that you'll get from increasing the carbohydrate in your diet, there is a health benefit as well. It comes in the form of fiber. Fiber is the nondigestible fraction of plant foods. When you eat whole grains, beans, vegetables, and fruits, you automatically eat a high-fiber diet. High-fiber diets have been found to be protective against the development of intestinal diseases, certain cancers, diabetes mellitus, and heart disease. A high-fiber diet will certainly keep your bowel regular, an important factor for an active person.

Your goal is to eat 65 percent of your calories as carbohydrate calories. This means making whole-grain and enriched breads and cereals, rice, buckwheat, potatoes, yams, beans, pastas, fruits, and vegetables the foundation of your diet. Without any more planning, your diet will be high in carbohydrate and low in fat, and full of all the important vitamins and minerals that you need to achieve peak performance every day.

FAT: THE NUTRIENT WE LOVE TO HATE

Depending on your total caloric intake, you have a minimum requirement of about 3 to 6 grams of fat per day. This means that on a 2,000- to 3,000-calorie diet, at least 1 to 2 percent of your calories must come from fat to avoid a dietary deficiency of fat. However, this does not mean that you will be in optimal health if you keep your fat intake this low.

Fat plays an essential role in your health and in your ability to perform. Fat is required for the manufacture of hormones; for the healthy maintenance of skin, hair, nerves, brain, and cell membranes; as padding around your organs to protect them from injury; and to transport fat-soluble vitamins from your food into and around your body. And as we mentioned earlier, fat is a critical fuel for exercise.

All of the concern about fat and the role it plays in promoting heart disease and cancer has caused many people to lower their fat intakes below what is considered a preventive level, and possibly below a healthy level. Many of my clients are on very low-fat diets when they first come to see me (SMK). Their fat intakes are usually around 10 percent of their calories. This low-fat intake causes several problems.

The first is that they are not getting enough of the fat-soluble vitamin E in their diet. Vitamin E is an important antioxidant that is a critical nutrient in a high-performance diet. It protects cells from damage caused by ultraviolet radiation, pollution, cigarette smoke, stress, and excessive exercise. This damage might lead to cancer and heart disease. (More about antioxidants in a later section.)

Second, their diets are so low in fat that they are not consuming enough calories to keep their energy levels high. Remember that during most of your exercise time, fat is the primary source of fuel. For young women, a very low-fat intake has been associated with a disruption or dysfunction of their normal menstrual patterns and can affect fertility.

We recommend that most people eat a diet that has 20 percent of its calories from fat. If you've been on a very low-fat diet, the first thing that you will notice when you add back a little fat is that you are enjoying your food more and feeling more satisfied. Satiety is one of the major functions of fat in food.

If you have been on a higher-fat diet, don't panic about how hard it might be to cut out the fat. Once you increase your carbohydrates and control your total calorie intake, it is easy to decrease the fat. It happens automatically. You are so full of starches and the extra fiber that comes along with them that there just isn't much room left for fat.

All of the recipes in this book have 30 percent or less of their calories from fat. By mixing and matching recipes with other foods, you can easily keep your dietary fat at 20 percent of your calories.

DIET, HEART DISEASE, AND CANCER

Fat is the greatest dietary culprit in raising blood cholesterol levels and promoting the risk of cancer. Dietary fats are the building blocks of cholesterol in our bodies. The amount of cholesterol in our diet does not influence blood levels of cholesterol as much as total fats in our diet, as well as certain types of fats.

There are several different kinds of fat. The fats we eat are described chemically as saturated or unsaturated. Unsaturated fats are further divided into two kinds: monounsaturated and polyunsaturated.

Saturated fats, those found mostly in beef, dairy products, commercially prepared baked goods, tropical oils (like coconut, palm, and palm-kernel oils), and the chemically altered hydrogenated oils found in margarines and shortenings, are the enemies in our diets contributing to high blood cholesterol and cancer risk.

Unsaturated fats, found in vegetable products, nuts, seeds, grains, and fish, are helpful in the fight against heart disease. The original research showed that poly-unsaturated fats, those found mostly in corn, sunflower, and safflower oils, were the most important for lowering total blood cholesterol and LDL, the "bad" cho-lesterol. But the polyunsaturated fats also lowered HDL, the "good" cholesterol. Not long afterward, cancer researchers found that not only was a high total fat intake linked to cancer risk, but a diet high in polyunsaturated fats increased the risk of certain cancers as well.

So scientists went back to the drawing board and found that monounsaturated fats—those found in olive oil; peanut oil; canola oil; and fish oils from salmon, mackerel, halibut, swordfish, black cod, rainbow trout, and shellfish are very heart-healthy fats. They help bring down total blood cholesterol and LDL cholesterol but don't lower HDL at the same time. The fish oils may have separate protective effects by decreasing the risk of stroke from blood clots. And fish oils are not associated with increased risks of cancer.

HOW TO COORDINATE YOUR FATS

There is no question that the total amount of fat in the diet should be less than 30 percent of your calorie intake. For a high-performance diet you should eat no more than 20 percent of your calories as fat. The makeup of that 20 percent should then come mostly from monounsaturated fats, secondarily from polyunsaturated fats, and lastly from saturated fats. By eating a high-carbohydrate diet and using the healthful oils suggested above, you will automatically create a diet that con-tains the right amounts of the different kinds of fats.

Because of the new research implicating hydrogenated oils (margarine) in the potential development of heart disease and cancers, we have not used any marga-rine in these recipes. Our most common choices of fat are healthful oils. Occa-sionally you will find a recipe calling for small amounts of butter instead of oil because in these particular recipes we feel that butter makes the food taste much better. Oil can be substituted for butter in these recipes, but we prefer the added flavor of butter with virtually no risk to your health in such small quantities.

If you use margarine, choose margarines that have a liquid oil as the first ingre-dient. This usually means avoiding stick margarines and selecting tub margarines, but you must still read the labels. Use low-fat and skim-milk dairy products, and eat mostly fish, seafood, skinless poultry, and small portions of beef.

FISH FAT FACTS

While some fish may be oilier than others, nutrition research has indicated that fish oils may be protective against heart disease and should frequently be included in our diets. A study of the Eskimos of Greenland revealed that despite a relatively high-fat diet, they have a very low incidence of heart disease and stroke. Thorough analysis of the data indicated that fish is the major source of fat in the Eskimo diet. It was associated not only with a low rate of heart disease but also with low plasma triglyceride levels and a relatively long blood-coagulation time (a protection against stroke).

Fish oils differ structurally from the fat of other animals. Fish oil contains the highly polyunsaturated omega-3 fatty acids found in the compounds EPA and DHA. The molecular structure of these compounds allows them to play a significant role in preventing blood clots and the buildup of plaque on arterial walls, both of which contribute to heart disease and stroke.

The benefits of seafood are numerous: it is one of the leanest sources of protein, it is an important source of vitamins and minerals, it is low in total and saturated fat, and it is the most abundant source of omega-3 fatty acids. Even fish and shellfish that are relatively high in total fat or cholesterol are valuable food choices because of their omega-3 fatty acid content.

Cold-water fish and shellfish are generally higher in omega-3 fatty acids. Fish such as halibut, salmon, sablefish, snapper, catfish, and rainbow trout are the best. Seafood such as shrimp, oysters, squid, and mussels are also good selections. Even albacore tuna packed in water is a valuable source of healthy fish oil.

For a heart-healthy diet, eat fish at least twice a week. We have selected some of our favorite fast and easy fish recipes that even the novice fish eater will love.

PROTEIN: IT WON'T PUMP YOU UP

Since the ancient Greeks trained to compete in the Olympic games, athletes have believed that they could build muscle by eating lots of meat. New scientific evidence shows that meat is not the magic ingredient of the muscle-building diet. Subjects who ate a high-carbohydrate, moderate-protein diet during strength training gained significantly more lean body mass than subjects who ate high-protein diets.

Muscle tissue is built from proteins, and there is a slight increase in the body's need for protein during strength training. But the protein requirement for building muscle is moderate compared to the energy required to build it. This is really the key to building muscle. Without an abundance of energy, muscles cannot grow in size or strength. The best source of energy for building muscle is carbohydrate.

In fact, endurance athletes have about the same protein requirements as muscle builders. During endurance exercise, some protein is used for energy along with carbohydrate and fat. Protein is not used as an energy source during strength-training exercise, but it is used for building muscle tissue. The net result is virtually an equivalent requirement for dietary protein in endurance athletes and body builders. If you are cross-training and including both strength and endurance exercises in your regimen, it is likely that you also have a slightly higher protein requirement.

But whether you are training for endurance, building muscle, or cross-training, a diet with 15 percent of its calories from protein will meet your protein needs. When you eat more protein than you need, your body must break off nitrogen from the extra amino acid molecules in order to make the molecules useful for energy metabolism. This process creates ammonia. Since ammonia is toxic to humans, it has to be changed into urea and excreted from the body, causing undue stress. And if you are eating too much protein you won't be consuming enough carbohydrate to keep your energy level high. Finally, since most good sources of protein also contain fat, you'll be eating too much fat as well.

Good Sources of Protein

Meat is an important part of a high-performance diet. Meat is a wonderful source of protein, as well as iron, zinc, thiamin, vitamin B-6, and vitamin B-12, all important nutrients in a high-performance diet. The trick to including meat in a high-performance diet is choosing low-fat cuts of meat and eating moderate portions.

When choosing beef, select the "skinny six": eye of round, round tip, top round, top loin, tenderloin, and sirloin. The "select" cut is always leanest. Always trim fat from meat before cooking. (The skin from poultry can be removed before or after cooking. But make sure to remove it.) Then brown the meat by broiling, grilling, or cooking in a nonstick pan with little or no oil.

Keep the serving size moderate. If your entrée is simply meat, about 3 ounces of cooked lean beef (start with 4 ounces of uncooked, boneless meat) is considered a moderate serving for a 2,000-calorie diet. A 3-ounce serving is about the size of a deck of cards or the palm of a woman's hand. For a 3,000-calorie diet, a 4- to 5-ounce serving is moderate (start with 5- to 6-ounces of raw meat).

As mentioned above, fish and seafood are also wonderful sources of protein. They are usually lower in fat than beef or chicken, and the fat is a healthful fat.

To meet the demands of the marketplace, pork producers have altered the genetics of pigs as well as their feed. As a result, pork today is leaner than in the past, with the leanest cuts coming from the loin and leg areas. You will find that the pork recipes here are very tasty and especially low in fat.

Don't forget dairy products. Low-fat and skim milk, cheeses, and eggs are fabulous sources of high-quality protein, as well as other very important minerals and vitamins like calcium and riboflavin. Since all the fat and cholesterol in an egg is found in the yolk, our recipes are light on egg yolks. You can decrease the fat and cholesterol when you are cooking your own recipes by replacing each egg yolk with two egg whites.

THE VEGETARIAN DIET

A well-balanced vegetarian-style diet is full of plant foods like fruits, vegetables, legumes (dried beans and peas), and whole-grain cereals. These foods are all naturally high in carbohydrate and low in fat, making the diet a perfect one for athletes. You can certainly be healthy and perform at peak levels, and be a vegetarian. We have included an entire chapter of delicious vegetarian recipes that will help meet your daily protein needs and keep your body running strong.

WATER: THE NUTRIENT THAT GETS NO RESPECT

Water makes up about 60 percent of an adult's body weight, and a higher percentage in children. We can live up to forty days without food, but we will die within seven days without water.

The fluids in our body form a heavily trafficked river through our arteries, veins, and capillaries, carrying nutrients to our cells and taking waste products away and out of the body. Fluids fill virtually every space in our cells and between cells. Water molecules not only fill space but help form the structures of macromolecules like proteins and glycogen. The chemical reactions that keep us alive occur in water, and water is an active participant in those reactions.

Water performs many other essential functions. As the primary fluid in our bodies, water serves as a solvent for minerals, vitamins, amino acids, glucose, and many other small molecules. Without water, we could not even digest these essential nutrients, let alone absorb, transport, and utilize them.

How Much Is Enough?

A 150-pound adult male carries about 45 quarts of fluid in his body; a 120-pound adult female carries about 36 quarts of fluid. Just while sitting in a temperate climate, the man will lose about 3 quarts of fluid a day through perspiration and excretion, and the woman will lose about 2½ quarts. In the desert, the same sedentary man can lose more than 10 quarts and the woman can lose more than 8 quarts a day.

When you exercise, you lose even more water. Depending on your size and how much you sweat, you lose about a quart (4 cups) of water per hour of exercise. Since "a pint's a pound the world around," every pound lost during exercise represents the loss of a pint, or 2 cups, of fluid.

If our 150-pound man loses 2 percent of his body water (6 cups, or 3 pounds), his physical and mental performance will drop by 20 percent. If he loses 4 percent of his body water (12 cups, or 6 pounds), his performance will drop by 30 percent and his health will be at risk.

The average person needs to drink 8 to 10 cups of water a day. If exercise and/or a hot and humid environment is added to average activity, the body's requirements for water increase.

Weigh yourself before and after exercise. Any weight lost during a workout is fluid loss, and it should be replaced by drinking 2 cups of water for every pound lost. It's helpful to drink water before and during exercise, so that dehydration does not occur during your workout.

SPORTS DRINKS

The sports drink selection has recently grown from just beverages designed to replace lost fluids, to drinks that increase your carbohydrate intake during exercise, and even those that add a significant amount of nutrients and calories to your diet.

The simple fluid replacers are basically water with a little sugar, salt, and potassium, and possibly a few other electrolytes. The additives help your body absorb water more quickly, and the sugar does provide a slight amount of energy. The next step up is the high-carbohydrate drink. These are packed with carbohydrates including sucrose, fructose, and dextrose polymers. The high-carbohydrate drink is really a carbohydrate supplement to be used when you can't eat enough carbohydrates to meet your daily needs, or to drink after exercise to replace glycogen stores. The third variety is a meal-replacement beverage. It is based on the instant-breakfast concept but is much higher in carbohydrates and calories than the original instant powdered breakfast drink.

Fluid-replacement sports drinks are very useful, especially if you dislike the taste of water while you exercise. They replenish your fluids as well as give you a little energy replacement. The beverage chapter of this book has our own unique sports drink formula (page 203). It is very close in content to the popular commercial fluid-replacement drinks, and we like it better because it doesn't have any artificial coloring. The Energizer recipe, also found in the beverage chapter (page 204), is designed to be a meal-replacement beverage. We have not tried to duplicate the high-carbohydrate drinks since the manufactured formulas are truly better than anything that we could design in our own kitchen.

THE ANTIOXIDANT ADVANTAGE

As you exercise and burn fuel for energy, your body produces chemicals called free radicals. The free radicals can cause cell damage (oxidation) that may be partly responsible for the effects of aging and certain diseases. Cigarette smoke, exhaust fumes, ultraviolet radiation, excessive sunlight, certain medications, stress, and strenuous exercise can cause an increase in the production of free radicals.

Your body has a natural defense mechanism of antioxidant chemicals that work to disarm the free radicals before they cause oxidative damage. But as you age or are exposed to external factors that make you mass-produce free radicals, your natural defenses may become overwhelmed. Without the healthy function of antioxidant chemicals to keep the free radicals in check, the damage caused can lead to advanced aging, degenerative disease, heart disease, and cancer.

The Hard Facts

The most recent news about antioxidants is the role that they may play in helping to prevent heart disease. By keeping the cholesterol in your bloodstream from becoming oxidized, the antioxidants may inhibit the buildup of plaque in the arteries. Without any plaque your arteries can't get blocked, and you avoid heart disease.

The results of two large research studies lend support to this theory. The two studies, one on women and one on men, found that those people who supplemented their diet with large doses of the natural antioxidant vitamin E had a decreased risk of developing coronary artery disease.

The development of cancer has also been tied to the amounts of two other natural antioxidants, vitamin C and beta-carotene, in the diet. More than a decade of research and more than 150 studies have produced evidence that eating fruits and vegetables rich in vitamin C or beta-carotene is linked with a reduced risk of many types of cancer.

Some very recent studies have looked at the effects of antioxidant supplementation on exercise performance. Although the results are still very preliminary and no thorough studies have been done, the evidence supports the theory that some athletes have greater requirements for antioxidants. Since increased exercise increases free radical production, the body requires more antioxidants to neutralize the extra free radicals.

The Natural Source

The natural source of antioxidant chemicals is the food that you eat. Vitamin E, vitamin C, and beta-carotene are used by the body to disarm the free radicals. The more of these vitamins that we eat in our food, the greater our antioxidant supply for fighting free radical damage.

Getting enough vitamin C and beta-carotene is easy. The best sources of vitamin C are citrus fruits and juices, berries, green and red peppers, broccoli, collard greens, tomatoes, potatoes, and spinach. The best sources of beta-carotene are orange and yellow vegetables and fruits, such as carrots, yams, squash, and cantaloupe, and green leafy vegetables like Swiss chard, kale, and broccoli.

Getting enough vitamin E in your diet may be tricky. Since vitamin E is fat soluble, the greatest source of vitamin E is vegetable oils and high-fat plant foods like wheat germ, nuts, and seeds. By cutting the fat out of your diet to get lean, you cut out some of the vitamin E at the same time.

That is why it is important to continue to include healthy oils in your diet and to use some wheat germ, nuts, and seeds as accompaniments to your meals. We have noted the recipes that are high in antioxidants. Choose at least one of these recipes every day, along with enjoying the raw fruits and vegetables that are such good sources of vitamin C and beta-carotene.

DESIGN YOUR OWN DIET

The key to the high-performance diet is the amount of carbohydrate that it contains. So let's design your diet around the amount of carbohydrate that you will need to eat every day to meet your energy needs.

The first step is to figure out how many calories you need to meet your basal metabolic requirements (energy needs at rest) and then add a factor to include your daily activity. Once your energy needs are determined, you will compute your carbohydrate requirement at 65 percent of your daily calories. Next, determine your protein requirement at 15 percent of your calories, and finally, compute your fat needs at 20 percent of your daily calories.

Turning all of these numbers into food is the next step. You might be aware that many people count fat grams rather than calories in order to lose weight. But by counting only fat grams, you place your focus on what you don't want to eat, rather than on what you do want to eat. We have a more positive approach. Count carbohydrate grams. Since this is a high-performance diet based on eating lots of carbohydrates, count your carbohydrate grams each day and make sure that you eat all of them.

If you concentrate your efforts on eating a high-carbohydrate diet, you will almost naturally end up eating moderate amounts of protein and small amounts of fat. Pay secondary attention to your protein grams to make sure that you are getting enough, and your fat grams will likely fall into place easily.

Use the nutrient analyses at the end of each recipe to determine how many grams of each nutrient you are getting from your meals. We have included a short list of foods that are high in carbohydrates and their gram amounts. You might find it helpful to purchase a basic pocket carbohydrate counter (the little guides sold at supermarket checkouts and in bookstores) to determine the carbohydrate content of commonly eaten foods when you are not using the recipes in this book.

Take the stress out of selecting your foods. Your diet is a combination of all the foods that you eat over a period of time, not just each specific food that you eat. Place your focus on balancing your foods throughout the day and over a period of a week, rather than targeting one food at a time. At one meal you might eat one high-fat food and three high-carbohydrate, low-fat foods. Even though you have included one high-fat food, the total combination is a high-carbohydrate, low-fat meal.

Determine Your Energy Needs

There are many ways to determine energy needs. There is a direct method, in which a person is put inside a special chamber where his or her actual energy usage can be measured. Since this method is impractical for daily clinical use, formulas have been developed that are based on the amount of muscle and fat on a person's body. When we are working with a client, we do body-fat skin-fold and muscle-circumference measurements to determine the amount of muscle and fat on that person's body. Then we calculate his or her energy requirements using several different types of formulas.

But even this level of sophistication isn't always possible, so shortcuts have been developed that work nearly as well. In fact, while working with the Cleveland Browns I (SMK) didn't always have time to determine energy needs using the time-consuming clinical measures. Sometimes I used a quick method that, when compared later to the longer calculations, came out extremely close to the more sophisticated technique.

Since it is unlikely that you have a sports nutritionist available to take your body measurements, and since the quick method works so well, we have chosen to use the quick method to help you determine your energy needs.

Step 1: Take your present weight and multiply by 10. If you are overfat, use what you consider to be your ideal body weight in place of your present weight. (Don't confuse *overfat* with *overweight*, since if you are muscular you might weigh more than what an ideal body-weight chart would suggest. Overfat is determined by your ability to pinch more than 1 inch of skin 2 inches above your belly button.) This number is the amount of calories that you need each day to perform the activities of rest: maintaining your heartbeat, breathing, and other basic metabolic functions.

Step 2: According to the chart below, multiply your present weight by the appropriate activity factor.

Step 3: Add together the quotients from steps 1 and 2.

Activity Factors for Determining Energy Needs

Sedentary	Moderately Active	Active	Very Active	Extremely Active
3	4	5	7	10

Sedentary: No exercise, gardening, or housework

Moderately Active: Exercises, gardens, does housework 3–5 times per week for 20–30 minutes per session. Uses stairs and walks briskly.

Active: Exercises 3–5 times per week for 60 minutes per session. Uses stairs and walks briskly.

Very Active: Exercises 3–5 times per week for 90-plus minutes per session, or has more than one 60-minute workout session per day. Uses stairs and walks briskly. Has other daily physical activity. Competitive recreational athletes often fit into this category.

Extremely Active: Exercises 5 or more times per week for 120–plus minutes per session, or has more than one 90-minute workout session per day. Uses stairs and walks briskly. Has other daily physical activity. Professional athletes often fit into this category.

Step 4: Adjust for your weight goal.

If you would like to lose weight, subtract 250–500 calories per day and increase your exercise to burn 250–500 calories each day. This should result in a weight loss of approximately 1 to 2 pounds per week. This may seem like a small amount of weight. But all of the research on weight loss has shown that the best way to lose weight *and keep it off* is to lose no more than 1 to 2 pounds per week. This method also helps you avoid feeling hungry and deprived, helping you to stay with your program.

If you need to gain weight, add 400–500 calories per day and increase muscle-resistance exercise. To gain 1 pound of muscle, it takes 2,500 calories and a lot of hard work. Since you don't want to put on fat while you're building muscle, you have to add just enough calories to meet your extra energy needs, and then build the muscle slowly. This method should result in a weight gain of about 1 pound per week. It may take several weeks before the increase in weight really shows.

Determine Your Carbohydrate Needs

Sixty-five percent of your calories should be carbohydrate calories. Once you have determined your total energy needs for the day, you can calculate the number of carbohydrate grams that you should be eating every day.

Step 1: Multiply your total daily calories by 65 percent (.65) to determine your daily calories from carbohydrate.

Step 2: Divide your daily carbohydrate calories by 4, the number of calories in each gram of carbohydrate. This is your total daily allotment of carbohydrate grams.

For example:

2,000 calories × .65 = 1,300

1,300 ÷ 4 = 325 grams total carbohydrate

Good Food Sources of Carbohydrates

Food	Amount	Carbohydrates (Grams)
FRUITS		
Apple	1 medium	20
Apricots, dried	8 halves	30
Banana	1 medium	25
Orange	1 medium	20
Raisins	¼ cup	30
VEGETABLES		
Baked potato	1 large	55
Broccoli	1 stalk	5
Carrot	1 medium	10
Green beans	½ cup	7
Peas	½ cup	10
Winter squash	½ cup	15
Zucchini	½ cup	4

continued

Food	Amount	Carbohydrates (Grams)
BREAD-TYPE FOODS		
Bagel	1 whole	30
Bran muffin	1 large	45
English muffin	1 whole	25
Graham cracker	2 squares	11
Granola bar	1 bar	13
Matzo	1 sheet	28
Pancakes	two 4-inch	30
Pita pocket	½ of 8-inch-round	22
Saltines	6	15
Submarine roll	8-inch	60
Waffle, toaster	1	17
Whole wheat, high-fiber bread	2 slices	35
BREAKFAST CEREALS		
Cream of Wheat	1 serving	22
Grape-Nuts	¼ cup	23
Granola	¼ cup	18
Oatmeal, maple instant	1 packet	30
Raisin bran	½ cup	21
BEVERAGES		
Apple juice	8 oz.	30
Apricot nectar	8 oz.	35
Cola	12 oz.	38
Cranberry-raspberry drink	8 oz.	36
Milk, chocolate	8 oz.	25
Milk, low-fat (2 percent)	8 oz.	13
Orange juice	8 oz.	25
GRAINS, PASTA, STARCHES		
Baked beans	1 cup	50
Lentils, cooked	1 cup	40
Ramen noodles	1 package	50

continued

Food	Amount	Carbohydrates (Grams)
Rice, cooked	1 cup	35
Spaghetti, cooked	1 cup	40
Stuffing	1 cup	40
ENTRÉES, CONVENIENCE FOODS		
Bean burrito	1	50
Chili	1 cup	45
Macaroni & cheese	1 cup	45
Pizza, cheese	2 slices	42
Split-pea soup	8 oz.	24
SWEETS, SNACKS, DESSERTS		
Chocolate-chip cookies	2	20
Cranberry sauce	2 T	15
Fig Newtons	2	22
Fruit yogurt	1 cup	50
Honey	1 T	15
Maple syrup	2 T	25
Soft ice cream	1 medium cone	35
Strawberry jam	1 T	13

Determine Your Protein Needs

Step 1: Multiply your total daily calories by 15 percent (.15) to determine your daily calories from protein.

Step 2: Divide your daily protein calories by 4, the number of calories in each gram of protein, to determine your total grams of protein per day.

For example:

2,000 calories × .15 = 300

300÷4 = 75 grams total protein

If you need more than 2,500 calories per day, or you would like a more accurate determination of your protein needs, use this formula:

Endurance Athletes: Your body weight in pounds × 0.5 = grams total protein

Strength Athletes: Your body weight in pounds × 0.7 = grams total protein

The **High Performance** Cookbook

Determine Your Fat Needs

Your total fat intake should be 20 percent of your daily calories. This low-fat diet should contain much more unsaturated than saturated fat (5 percent saturated, 8 percent monounsaturated, 7 percent polyunsaturated).

One way to monitor your fat intake is by counting the fat grams in your diet. You can calculate your own suggested daily fat intake by using the following formulas.

For total fat:

Step 1: Multiply your total daily calories by 20 percent (.20) to determine your daily calories from fat.

Step 2: Divide your daily fat calories by 9, to determine your total daily grams from fat. (There are 9 calories in each gram of fat.)

> For example:
> 2,000 calories × .20 = 400
> 400 ÷ 9 = 44 grams total fat

For saturated fatty acids (SFA):

Step 1: Multiply your total daily calories by 5 percent (.05) to determine your daily calories from SFA.

Step 2: Divide your daily SFA calories by 9, to determine your total daily grams of SFA. (There are 9 calories in each gram of fat.)

> For example:
> 2,000 calories × .05 = 100
> 100 ÷ 9 = 11 grams SFA

Once you have calculated your own dietary allowance for total fat and saturated fat, you need to use the nutrient analyses at the bottom of the recipes and read food labels for the fat content per serving of the foods that you buy in the supermarket. The total fat and saturated fat grams are listed under "Nutrition Facts" on any food package that provides a nutrition label. Make sure, if you are tallying the grams of fat from one serving, that you eat only one serving of the food.

CHAMPIONS EAT BREAKFAST

Just as the commercials say, breakfast is the most important meal of the day. Unfortunately it gets little respect, and many people with fast-paced lives skip breakfast. If this describes you, now is the time to change that habit forever. Your metabolism slows down after an overnight fast, and the only way to get it going full speed again is to feed it. Breakfast gives you a burst of energy that lasts all day.

Although breakfast is most enjoyable eaten at the table at a leisurely pace, it's okay to eat breakfast in your car, waiting for the bus, or on the train. We've included many one-minute breakfasts that are sure to fit your hurry-up morning schedule.

MEAL MISSERS

If you skip meals regularly, there is no way that you'll be able to perform at top speed. You just won't have the energy available to keep going. Many of the recipes here can be packed up and taken with you to work for lunch. Change your meal-skipping habit by seeing how quick and easy these recipes are to make. Many of them don't take much longer than our one-minute breakfasts.

When you know you don't have time for a full meal, or if you have trouble getting in all the calories that you need in a day, our Energizer drink, found in the beverage chapter (page 204), packs a powerful punch and can remedy your energy deficit.

THE END OF DEPRIVATION

Thought you could never eat cheesecake again? Think again. We have included a wonderful cheesecake recipe in the desserts chapter (page 184) that meets all the qualifications of a high-performance food. Try it and all the other wonderful treats to keep your sweet tooth satisfied.

The words *guilt* and *deprivation* are not part of the high-performance vocabulary. But *balance* is a very important word. As long as you keep your fat intake low most of the time, you can splurge and occasionally enjoy a higher-fat food, and the total fat calories will balance out.

ON THE ROAD

When your energy requirements are high, it is best to eat more than just three big meals a day. Your body works most efficiently if you eat less at each meal but eat more frequently throughout the day. This means that snacking is important even if you have to eat on the go. Design your diet to allow for three small meals and several snacks that you can pack every day.

The high-performance snack recipes can be enjoyed at home or on the road. Most of them will do just as well traveling on the freeway in your car or carried on the trail in your backpack.

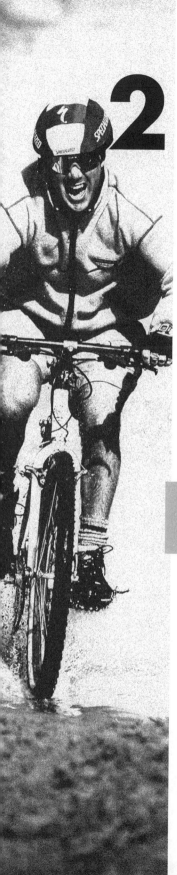

the High-Performance KITCHEN

T here is nothing supernatural about being a good cook. Most good cooks will tell you that their secret is having the right foods and the right utensils on hand and, of course, following directions. Getting the first two parts right usually takes some experience and some planning. We're going to give you a primer that you can use in lieu of experience so you can enter your high-performance kitchen with a leg up.

IT'S ALL IN THE PLANNING

Planning ahead is the key. You can meet your high-performance nutritional demands, even with your hectic schedule, if you just think ahead and stock your shelves and fridge with some important items.

Pots and Pans

Your life will be easier if you have a large pot for cooking pasta and several smaller saucepans, a stove-top or electric wok, a microwave oven, a broiler or gas grill, a toaster oven (useful but not absolutely necessary), two 1-quart and two 1-pint oven-safe casseroles, an 8-inch-square microwave-safe and oven-safe pan, a nonstick frying pan (it can double as a wok), and a nonstick cookie sheet.

Other Kitchen Gadgets

There are a million and one kitchen gadgets, and every cook has his or her own preferences. To make your life in the kitchen as easy as possible, we suggest that you have the following standard items: a blender, a small food processor, a hand-held electric mixer, a colander, a yogurt strainer or cheesecloth, and several plastic storage containers with lids for storing leftovers and taking food on the road.

In Your Pantry

When you have the right staples on hand, you can usually come up with something to make for a meal, even when you thought you had nothing to eat in the house. We do it all the time, and many of these recipes are based on exactly that concept.

Nonperishable items that should always be in your cupboard are brown rice and parboiled brown rice, bulgur wheat, buckwheat, a variety of pastas, canned low-salt chicken stock, sun-dried tomatoes, raisins, tomato paste, canned whole tomatoes with no added salt, low-salt tomato juice, unbleached all-purpose flour, whole-wheat flour, unsweetened cocoa, cornstarch, granulated sugar, brown sugar, honey, molasses, a variety of vegetable oils (our favorites are canola, olive, sesame, peanut, and sunflower), nonstick vegetable oil spray (there are several flavors), balsamic vinegar, red and white wines to cook with, and fat-free salad dressing.

Store soy sauce, Worcestershire sauce, hot sauce, Tabasco, lemon juice, barbecue sauce, catsup, mustard, low-fat mayonnaise, unsweetened applesauce, and pasta sauce in your refrigerator after they are opened, and try to keep an extra of each on hand in your cupboard. If you won't be using up an entire bottle of an unsaturated oil (like canola) within a couple of weeks, you should keep it refrigerated.

A note about soy sauce: Some of our recipes suggest low-sodium soy sauce instead of the regular high-sodium variety. We keep both kinds on hand. Some recipes just don't taste the same with the low-sodium substitute. We also have a strong recommendation about cooking wine: use a wine that is good enough to drink. Products designated as "cooking wine" have added salt and are not recommended.

Never run out of fresh ginger and fresh garlic. Many supermarkets now stock minced ginger and garlic in jars. These are time-savers, but they don't have the zing of fresh. Fresh peeled garlic cloves can also be found in the fancy produce section of some supermarkets. These taste just as good as the garlic you peel yourself. You might keep some of the prepared ginger and garlic around for those times when every minute counts.

You'll find fresh Parmesan cheese in many of the recipes. Just a little adds so much flavor. Most grocery stores sell it already shredded or grated. Keep some in your fridge, and don't use a canned version. It just won't do the food justice.

Shredded fat-free cheeses and grated Parmesan cheese can be kept in the freezer to extend their shelf life. They will still work just great in recipes.

On Your Spice Rack

A good variety of herbs and spices can go a long way in adding flavor to your diet. Remember that dried spices are three times stronger than fresh. Always have:

basil	bay leaves	black pepper
cardamom	chili powder	chives
cinnamon	crushed red pepper	cumin
dillweed	marjoram	nutmeg
oregano	paprika	red cayenne pepper
rosemary	sage	salt
salt-free herb/ vegetable seasoning mix	tarragon	thyme white pepper

IN AND AROUND THE FRIDGE

No high-performance kitchen would be complete without a stock of potatoes and onions. We always keep a variety of potatoes in a basket: red-skinned potatoes, baking potatoes, and the new delicious Yukon gold or butter potatoes. The Yukon gold taste like they've already got butter on them when you eat them just plain.

Try to keep a variety of frozen and fresh foods on hand. Precut fresh and frozen vegetables for stir-fries and salads are a must. Carrots and fresh parsley are also great to have around. We use them in many of the recipes.

Frozen shrimp and crabmeat are great to have for those nights when you can't get out to buy fresh fish. Precut chicken and beef for stir-fries are also useful time-savers, but you have to either use them within three days of purchase or put them in the freezer for up to nine months.

When you find good, fresh tofu, buy two pounds. Tofu will stay fresh in your refrigerator for two weeks as long as you change the water every other day. The packaged brands of tofu stay fresh for a very long time and are useful in some recipes, but they don't have the same taste as fresh.

It's easy to throw several of our recipes together if you keep a stock of fresh dairy products. Nonfat or low-fat plain yogurt, nonfat or low-fat sour cream, low-fat or skim milk, low-fat cottage or ricotta cheese, and eggs will help make your menu planning a breeze.

KEEPING THE LID ON YOUR VITAMINS AND MINERALS

After you've gone to the trouble to purchase the freshest and most healthful foods, it's important to store them and cook them properly so that you don't lose their wonderful attributes.

Nutrient Destruction

Certain nutrients are very sensitive to exposure to heat, light, water, and oxygen. No matter how careful you are with your cooking methods, cooking of any kind destroys some nutrients. In fact, as soon as fruits and vegetables are harvested they begin to lose some of their nutrients.

By the time food reaches your plate, the total amount of nutrients lost will depend on how the food was handled before and after you bought it, its freshness, how well it was wrapped, the size of the pieces it was cut into, how long you cooked it, in how much water, and at what temperature. If food is handled and cooked using the best nutrient preservation techniques, the amount of nutrients lost is insignificant.

Nutrient Preservation

When food is prepared, some nutrients are destroyed and some are leached into the surrounding cooking medium. Thiamin, riboflavin, and vitamin C are easily destroyed by heat, and many other vitamins will break down after exposure to extremely hot temperatures for long periods of time. Since the conventional method of frying exposes foods to very high temperatures for extended time periods, and since it is also a high-fat cooking method, it is not recommended as a regular cooking style for a high-performance diet.

Exposure to high temperatures for very short periods of time can cook foods thoroughly and still preserve their nutrient integrity. Stir-frying is a very quick cooking method, so it causes far less destruction of vitamins than does regular frying. And since it requires very little oil, it is low in fat.

Many vitamins, and some minerals, will leach into cooking water. The more the food is exposed to water, the greater the leaching that occurs. But there are many steps that can be taken to avoid high nutrient losses due to leaching.

As with heat exposure, you should cook foods in water for the shortest time possible. Use small rather than large amounts of water, and cover pots or pans to speed cooking time. The fastest cooking methods are microwaving, steaming, and stir-frying.

When you cook or reheat foods in a microwave oven, make sure to follow the instructions for cooking times. Because cooking times are so short, there is high nutrient preservation with microwaving. But if food is overcooked, the nutrient content will be diminished.

Peels left on vegetables can help protect against leaching. Also, the less surface area exposed to water, the less leaching that will occur. Scrub produce well, cook it whole or in large rather than small chunks, and leave it unpeeled whenever possible.

Because exposure to air, or oxygen, can also destroy some vitamins, precut produce will lose more nutrients than whole. Make sure that any cut produce you do buy, and any you store in your refrigerator at home, is well wrapped and sealed, and use it within two days of purchase. To avoid major losses of water-soluble vitamins, don't immerse fruits or vegetables in water when storing.

Some vegetables are best prepared by boiling. When boiling, use only enough water to barely cover the vegetables. Bring the water to a full boil before adding the vegetables, and make sure to cover the pot during boiling.

One exception to the covered-pot rule are vegetables from the cruciferous family, like broccoli, cabbage, and cauliflower. These vegetables have high sulfur content. When the cooking medium is water, they are usually best prepared by boiling with the lid open or off the pot to allow the volatile sulfur flavors to escape.

Always time cooking vegetables. Cook them until they are just soft, yet still crisp and colorful. If you cook vegetables until they are limp and gray, they've lost not only flavor, texture, and eye appeal, but nutrients as well.

Whenever you cook foods in water, even when steaming, you will lose some nutrients. Just look at the cooking water the next time you boil or steam vegetables. Some of the color that you see is from nutrients leached during cooking. You can recover those nutrients by saving the cooking water and using it as a base for a soup or gravy. That way, you lose none of the nutrients at all.

There are still a few more tips to help you preserve the highest nutritional value in your foods. Cook foods as close to serving time as possible. The longer they are heated, or exposed to air, the more nutrients that are destroyed.

If you can't shop frequently, and fresh produce sits and wilts in your refrigerator before you can eat it, you've lost many of the nutrients before you ever begin to prepare the food for a meal. Contrary to popular belief, frozen fruits and vegetables are fresher and retain their nutrients better than wilted, improperly handled, and poorly stored "fresh" produce. When buying frozen fruits and vegetables, read labels. Avoid syrups and high-fat and high-salt cream sauces. You should be able to find plain frozen fruits, or fruits in light syrup or unsweetened juice, and plain frozen vegetables.

Just as with vegetables, nutrient losses from meats are greatest when preparation involves high temperatures and long cooking times. There is much less nutrient loss during broiling, grilling, and stir-frying than during roasting and baking. Broiling, grilling, and stir-frying are also low-fat methods of preparing meats, so you can achieve two goals at the same time.

NUTRIENT PERSPECTIVE

It is very important to keep in mind that even though some nutrients are lost during food handling and preparation, not all are lost. The amount of lost vitamins and minerals may be insignificant compared to the amount that remains.

Of course, you always want to get as much out of your food as you can and strive for optimal nutritional quality. Follow these few tips to help keep nutrients in and fat out, and you will be eating to your heart's, and body's, content.

Basic Rules for Cooking Vegetables in Water:

1. Bring water (salted or unsalted) to a boil before adding vegetables.
2. Return the water to a boil as quickly as possible.
3. Cook in barely enough water to prevent scorching, and put a lid on the pan. (Do not cover cruciferous vegetables like broccoli, Brussels sprouts, cabbage, and cauliflower because the color and flavor will suffer.)
4. Cook the vegetables only until barely done.
5. Serve promptly.

WHAT WE MEAN WHEN WE SAY...

Barbecue.   Roasting foods on a rack or a spit over coals is a fun, lower-fat way to prepare meat, poultry, fish, and even tofu and vegetables. Barbecuing gives a distinctive smoked flavor to foods. Trim fat from meat to prevent flare-up of flames and to reduce calories. If you are using a sauce to season the food, cook the food until almost done before saucing it.

Boil or stew.   This is a low-fat method of cooking foods in hot liquids. Starchy or root vegetables such as potatoes, corn on the cob, lima beans, and turnips are often boiled.

Broil.   Broiling is a quick way of cooking foods under direct heat without added fat. It's great for poultry, fish, and tender cuts of meat. Use a broiling pan or rack set in a shallow pan to allow fat to drain away. If basting, use lemon juice, fruit juice, or broth for flavor. Vegetables like onions, zucchini, and tomatoes can also be broiled.

Microwave.   Microwaving cooks foods faster than most other methods. You don't need to add fat to meat, poultry, or fish, and you use little or no water for vegetables. Microwaving is an excellent way to retain vitamins and color in vegetables. Since the power of microwave ovens varies, follow the manufacturer's directions for best results.

Roast or bake.   Roasting takes somewhat longer than other methods but requires little work on your part. Poultry and tender cuts of meat may be roasted. Cook in the oven, uncovered, on a rack in a shallow roasting pan, to allow fat to drain and permit heat to circulate around the meat. Potatoes, sweet potatoes, winter squashes, and onions can be baked. Simply wash, prick skins, and place vegetables on a baking sheet in the oven.

Sauté. The traditional method is to fry lightly in a little fat. We have minimized the amount of fat usually used to sauté but the results are just as delicious. Just about any food can be sautéed, but we limit its use to where it really brings out a flavor in a way that no other method can, such as in the preparation of garlic, onions, and mushrooms.

Steam. This is a great method for cooking vegetables without using fat. It works well for frozen and fresh vegetables such as asparagus, carrots, peas, and summer squash. Use a vegetable steamer or colander to hold the vegetables. Place the steamer in a pot with a little boiling water and cover. You can also use a covered microwave-safe dish and two tablespoons of water on high power in your microwave. To preserve color and vitamins, cook until the vegetables are just tender.

Stir-fry. Quick and easy, stir-frying requires relatively little fat and preserves the crisp texture and bright color of vegetables. Heat a wok or heavy skillet over very high heat, add just enough oil to lightly coat the bottom of the pan, add the food, and stir constantly while cooking. Start with thin strips or diced portions of meat, poultry, or fish. When the meat is almost done, add small pieces of vegetables such as broccoli, cauliflower, zucchini, bean sprouts, carrots, mushrooms, tomatoes, or green onions.

FAT SUBSTITUTION SOLUTIONS

There are ways to lower the fat content of many of the dishes that you love to make but know are too high in fat. You might find some of those recipes in this cookbook. If you'd like to try to alter other recipes on your own, here are a few tips. But remember, some recipes just don't work when they are made with fat substitutes. If a high-fat recipe can't be altered to fit your taste, don't change it. Eat the original version on special occasions, and enjoy it.

Instead of . . .	Use . . .
Butter	If the flavor is essential, use butter in small amounts; otherwise use soft tub margarine with liquid vegetable oil as the first ingredient
Cheese (high-fat)	Skim milk or light cheese; look for cheeses with less than 5 grams fat per ounce
Ice cream	Ice milk, frozen low-fat yogurt
Mayonnaise	light or nonfat mayonnaise, or combine nonfat yogurt and low-fat cottage cheese
Salad dressing	Low-fat salad dressing. Reduce the oil in homemade dressings by substituting water, vinegar, or lemon juice

continued

Instead of ...	Use ...
Saturated fats (coconut oil, palm oil, butter, lard)	Corn, safflower, sesame, cottonseed, sunflower, canola, soybean, olive oil
Soups	Chill broths, remove solidified fat, and reheat
Sour cream	Nonfat sour cream or low-fat yogurt, or blend $1/2$ cup low-fat cottage cheese with $1^1/_2$ teaspoons lemon juice
Whipped cream	Chill and whip evaporated skim milk
Whole egg	2 egg whites or an egg substitute
Whole milk	Skim, 1%, or 2% milk

FAT-CUTTING MEASURES FOR YOUR MAIN DISHES

Choose leaner meat, poultry, and fish:

Beef—round, loin, sirloin, and chuck (arm) steaks or roasts, especially "select" grade cuts
Pork—tenderloin, center loin roasts and chops, ham
Veal—other than ground
Lamb—leg, loin roasts and chops, foreshank
Chicken and turkey—remove the skin and visible fat
Most fish
Shellfish

Before cooking meat, poultry, and fish:

Trim visible fat.
Remove skin from poultry.

When cooking meat, poultry, and fish:

Place meat on a rack when roasting or broiling so that fat can drain away from the meat.

Cook with little or no added fat, using nonstick pans and cooking spray. Drain off fat before mixing in other ingredients.

Baste with unsalted broth, unsalted tomato juice, or fruit juice rather than with fatty drippings.

In preparing sauces and toppings:

Chill drippings and broth and remove fat before making gravies, soups, and sauces. You can also purchase a fat-skimmer at a kitchen gadgets store.

To avoid lumps, mix thickener (flour or cornstarch) with cold liquid ingredients (unsalted broth, water, fruit juice) before heating.

Make your own low-fat bread crumbs for toppings by drying bread in the microwave and crumbling it in the blender. Add your own favorite seasonings for extra flavor.

Try alternatives:

Boost the carbohydrate content of your main courses by combining them with pasta, rice, other grains, or vegetables.

Use only one egg yolk per serving in egg dishes. Make larger servings by adding extra egg whites, as in scrambled eggs. Use two egg whites for every yolk that you remove.

Prepare dishes made with cooked dried beans or peas, and use tofu in place of meat, poultry, or fish. This will boost your carbohydrates and lower your fats in one fell swoop.

COOKING WITH GRAINS

If you buy grains in boxes, cooking instructions are usually printed on the box. But if you buy them in bulk, you are on your own to figure out the correct cooking times and the right proportions of grain and water. Here is a list that should be very helpful as you learn to add more grains to your diet.

Cooking Times and Proportions for Select Grains

Grain	Water	Cooking Time	Yield
($1/2$ cup dry measure)			
Brown rice	1 cup	1 hour	$1^1/2$ cups
Buckwheat (kasha)	1 cup	15 minutes	$1^1/4$ cups
Bulgur wheat	1 cup	15–20 minutes	$1^1/4$ cups
Coarse cornmeal (polenta)	2 cups	25 minutes	$1^1/2$ cups
Cracked wheat	1 cup	25 minutes	$1^1/8$ cups
Millet	$1^1/2$ cups	45 minutes	$1^3/4$ cups
Parboiled brown rice	$2/3$ cup	10 minutes	1 cup

STORAGE TIPS AND GUIDELINES

Believe it or not, not all vegetables should be stored in the refrigerator, and there is a way to keep fresh ginger from shriveling up and dying before you get to use all of it. Take the little bit of extra time to follow these storage tips, and your fresh foods will last longer, look better, taste better, and retain more nutrient value.

Root vegetables like potatoes, yams, onions, turnips, and parsnips, along with winter squash, should be kept unrefrigerated and away from light and heat. This will help them stay firm for longer and will discourage sprouting. Tomatoes too, although not a root vegetable, retain their flavor longer when kept outside the fridge. Buy tomatoes in small enough quantities to use up before spoiling, and avoid refrigeration.

Unripe fruits should be left to ripen at room temperature and then refrigerated. Some fruits, such as grapes and watermelon, will not ripen further after picking. Bananas should not be refrigerated because it causes the skin to blacken. Whole pineapple should also not be refrigerated.

Garlic has its own unique storage needs. It's worthwhile to purchase a terracotta garlic keeper to keep your garlic dry in the refrigerator. It will last six to seven months in the coldest part of the fridge. Garlic can also be left unrefrigerated, as on a garlic strand that is hung in the kitchen.

Mushrooms should be kept unwashed and refrigerated in a terracotta keeper or wrapped in paper towels that are changed once they become damp. The purpose of all this is to keep them dry; mushrooms are fungi which absorb water readily, and water absorption promotes spoilage. Keeping away the dampness will help keep mushrooms fresh for ten to fourteen days. Never store mushrooms in plastic wrap. To prepare mushrooms, do not wash them. Wipe them clean with a paper towel or a mushroom brush. If you like, you can remove the outer skin layer to reveal a perfectly white mushroom.

A Chinese friend taught us how to store fresh ginger for nearly forever: Rinse the outside of the ginger. Slice it in half with the skin and place it in a small container, adding enough rice wine or sherry to cover the ginger. Keep it covered in the refrigerator, and you will use up the ginger before it spoils.

Dried herbs and spices don't stay fresh forever, although you might keep them in your cupboard for that long. To extend the shelf life of herbs and spices, keep them in closed containers away from light and heat. Whole spices like cloves, nutmeg, and peppercorns stay fresh for much longer. Grind them with a small hand-held processor, and you will notice a delicious difference between the preground and freshly ground flavors. If you've had herbs and spices hanging around for longer than one year, do your cooking a favor and buy fresh.

FOOD SAFETY

Unfortunately, we must assume that poultry and eggs are contaminated with salmonella; that raw fish contains bacteria, the hepatitis microbe, and other toxins; and that beef can be contaminated with the bacteria clostridium and E. coli (responsible for deadly hamburger incidents). Finally, undercooked pork can be contaminated with the trichinosis parasite. The guidelines below are meant to prevent intestinal upset or in some cases death from foodborne infections. All of our recipes recommend cooking food thoroughly. We are aware that at upscale restaurants, fish cooked rare, or raw fish or meat such as sushi and steak tartare,

are culinary delights. We used to enjoy all these foods but we think that it is an unnecessary risk to eat this way anymore. We recommend that for your health you avoid uncooked and undercooked foods as well.

Guidelines

1. Use plastic or glass cutting boards. Do not use wood cutting boards, especially for animal products. Some research has shown that wood boards can be safer (more resistant to bacteria) than plastic, but the best advice is to wash your cutting board in the dishwasher or with soap and hot water after every use, and you can only do that with a plastic or glass board, so that's what we recommend.
2. Do not use the same cutting board for raw and cooked animal products. Cut vegetables and fruits on a board different from the one you use for meats.
3. Cook animal foods, including fish, poultry, eggs, and meat, until well done (165°F to 212°F). Avoid eating raw animal products like sushi, oysters, and steak tartare.
4. Do not eat leftovers more than three days old unless they have been frozen. Thaw frozen food in the refrigerator, not on the counter.
5. Avoid cracked eggs or foods made with raw eggs such as homemade mayonnaise, eggnog, Caesar salad dressing, or hollandaise sauce. Use pasteurized egg products instead.
6. Wash all fruits and vegetables thoroughly.
7. Store partially used canned foods, including juices, in glass or plastic containers.

Storage Guide for Perishable Food
Refrigerated Items

Use Within:	Days	Weeks	Months
FRESH FRUITS			
Apples			1
Apricots, bananas, grapes, nectarines, peaches, pears, plums, watermelon	3–5		
Berries, cherries	2–3		
Cranberries, melons (except watermelon)		1	
FRESH VEGETABLES			
Beans (snap or wax), cauliflower, celery, cucumber, eggplant, green peppers, salad greens, tomatoes		1	
Beets, carrots, parsnips, radishes, rutabagas, turnip		2	
Broccoli, Brussels sprouts, greens (spinach, kale, collards, etc.), okra, green onions, peas, summer squash	3–5		

continued

Use Within:	Days	Weeks	Months
Cabbage, in crisper			1–2
Cabbage		1–2	
Corn, in husk	As soon as possible		

MEATS

	Days	Weeks	Months
Roasts, steaks, chops	3–5		
Ground meat, poultry, fish, variety meats	1–2		
Cooked meats and meat dishes	3–4		
Gravy and broth	1–2		

MILK PRODUCTS AND EGGS

	Days	Weeks	Months
Milk		1	
Cottage cheese	5–7		
Hard cheeses	several		
Eggs (in shell)		5	

Frozen Items

For Best Quality, Use Within:	Months
Fruits and fruit juice concentrates	12
Vegetables	8
Bread and yeast rolls	3

MEAT

	Months
Ground beef	3–4
Beef roasts and steaks	6–12
Lamb roasts	6–9
Pork roasts	4–8
Pork chops	3–4
Cooked meat dishes	2–3

POULTRY

	Months
Chicken parts	9
Turkey parts	6
Chicken or turkey, whole	12
Cooked chicken or turkey	4–6

FISH

	Months
Fish fillets	2–3
Cooked fish	3

DAIRY

	Months
Ice cream or sherbet	1

The **High-Performance** Cookbook

Table of Equivalent Measures

a pinch	$1/8$ teaspoon or less
3 teaspoons	1 tablespoon
4 tablespoons	$1/4$ cup
8 tablespoons	$1/2$ cup
2 cups	1 pint
4 cups	1 quart
4 quarts	1 gallon
16 ounces (weight)	1 pound
32 ounces (liquid)	1 quart
8 ounces (liquid)	1 cup
1 ounce (liquid)	2 tablespoons

Hot and Cold STARTERS Soups and Salads

Creamy Dill Soup ➤

This creamy, rich soup from Eastern Europe is quite wonderful and makes a truly unique treat. The unusual blend of dill and paprika will have your taste buds singing a Hungarian rhapsody. The sodium and potassium content of this soup makes it an excellent electrolyte replacer.

Nonstick cooking spray
2 medium onions, chopped
6 ounces mushrooms, sliced
¹/₂ cup chicken stock
¹/₂ teaspoon dillweed
1 teaspoon soy sauce
2 teaspoons paprika
¹/₂ cup skim milk
2 tablespoons cornstarch dissolved in 2 ounces or ¹/₄ cup cold water
2 ounces nonfat yogurt
1 teaspoon lemon juice
Salt and freshly ground black pepper to taste

1. Heat a nonstick skillet on high for 30 seconds to 1 minute. Spray the skillet with cooking spray. Add the onions and mushrooms to the pan. Stir often to prevent sticking.

2. After about 5 minutes, when the onions begin to soften, add the chicken stock along with the dillweed, soy sauce, and paprika. Simmer on low for 5 minutes.

3. Add the milk and the cornstarch mixture. Cook an additional 5 minutes, until the soup thickens. Add the yogurt and lemon juice. Add salt and pepper to taste.

For 2 servings each serving contains				
Calories	177	Fat	2g
Protein	26g	Cholesterol	4mg
Carbohydrates	30g	Sodium	1,577mg

For 3 servings each serving contains				
Calories	118	Fat	1g
Protein	17g	Cholesterol	3mg
Carbohydrates	20g	Sodium	1,051mg

Vegetable Chowder ➤

It doesn't matter if you just stepped off a New England lobster trawler or walked into your house after a heavy workout. This soup resembles a classic chowder—it will warm you up and give you thoughts of a day in New England. It will also load you up on vitamins A and C and folic acid and provide about 20 percent of your vitamin B requirements.

Nonstick cooking spray

1 small onion, chopped

2 large red-skinned potatoes, chopped

2 medium stalks celery (with leaves), chopped

2 medium carrots, chopped

1 teaspoon parsley flakes

2 cups water

2 ounces uncooked small egg noodles

1 tablespoon unsalted butter

1 cup skim milk

1 tablespoon cornstarch dissolved in $^1/_4$ cup cold water

Salt and freshly ground black pepper to taste

1. Heat a nonstick pot for 30 seconds to 1 minute. Spray with cooking spray. Heat for 1 minute. Add the onion and cook until it begins to soften, about 5 minutes.

2. Add the potatoes, celery, carrots, parsley, and water and bring to a boil over high heat. Add the uncooked noodles, butter, and milk. When the butter has melted, add the cornstarch mixture. Stir thoroughly. Cook the soup until the noodles are tender. Add salt and black pepper to taste.

For 2 servings
each serving contains

Calories	358	Fat	8g
Protein	12g	Cholesterol	45mg
Carbohydrates	62g	Sodium	146mg

For 3 servings
each serving contains

Calories	239	Fat	5g
Protein	8g	Cholesterol	30mg
Carbohydrates	41g	Sodium	97mg

"Alota Onions" Soup ➤

Whenever I've shared this recipe with anyone, the description has always started out with "a lot of onions." The water and sodium content makes it a great fluid replacer after exercise. This recipe, which serves only two or three, is pared down from the army-size version we make at home. Use it as the center of your meal. (SMK)

2 cloves fresh garlic, minced
¹/₂ tablespoon canola oil
¹/₂ tablespoon sesame oil
1¹/₂ large yellow onions, thinly sliced
6 cups water
1¹/₂ tablespoons soy sauce
¹/₄ teaspoon freshly ground black pepper
2 thick slices crisp French bread (3 slices for 3 servings)
4 teaspoons grated Parmesan cheese

1. Sauté the garlic in the oils in a shallow nonstick pan over medium heat until slightly soft, about 3 to 5 minutes. Add onions and cook, stirring occasionally, until slightly caramelized, about 20 minutes.

2. Transfer the onions and garlic to a soup pot. Add the water, soy sauce, and pepper. Bring to a low boil over high heat, then reduce the heat to low and simmer uncovered for 15 minutes.

3. Serve with 1 slice of bread at the bottom of each bowl. Sprinkle each full bowl with 2 teaspoons of Parmesan cheese for 2 servings. For 3 servings, sprinkle with 1¹/₃ teaspoons per bowl.

For 2 servings each serving contains				
Calories	311	Fat	9g
Protein	9g	Cholesterol	4mg
Carbohydrates	49g	Sodium	1,067mg

For 3 servings each serving contains				
Calories	241	Fat	7g
Protein	7g	Cholesterol	3mg
Carbohydrates	39g	Sodium	779mg

Beef Vegetable Noodle Soup ➤

This is one of my family's favorite soups. We eat it as a meal with just the addition of a great bread. It is a terrific choice following winter outdoor sports. I often add green beans and lima beans to the mixed vegetables, so just use your imagination. This soup is high in vitamins A and C, folic acid, and potassium. (KRFK)

4 ounces lean beef, cubed

Nonstick vegetable oil spray

8 ounces frozen mixed vegetables (peas, carrots, and corn are recommended)

1 cup (8 ounces) puréed tomatoes

2 cups water

2 ounces uncooked pasta (small shells or elbows work well)

Salt and freshly ground black pepper to taste

1. Before cubing the beef, trim any visible fat. If your beef had a bone, save it to toss into the soup.

2. Heat a nonstick empty pot on high for 30 seconds to 1 minute. Lightly coat the nonstick pot with cooking spray. Add the cubed beef and brown it, stirring often to prevent sticking.

3. When the beef is browned, after 5 minutes, add the frozen vegetables, puréed tomatoes, water, and pasta. Bring the pot to a boil and cook 10 to 15 minutes, or until the pasta is tender.

4. Add salt and pepper to taste.

For 2 servings each serving contains				
Calories	317	Fat	5g
Protein	21g	Cholesterol	28mg
Carbohydrates	49g	Sodium	128mg

For 3 servings each serving contains				
Calories	211	Fat	4g
Protein	14g	Cholesterol	19mg
Carbohydrates	33g	Sodium	86mg

Gazpacho ➤

This traditional Spanish soup really packs a zing and is truly easy to toss together. It will help you pack in vitamins A and C as well as potassium. Cold soups are a staple of summer but can be served year-round. The longer a food remains in contact with Tabasco, the spicier it gets. If preparing in advance, go light on the Tabasco; you can always add more.

³/₄ cucumber, peeled
1 medium ripe tomato
1 scallion
1¹/₂ cups unsalted tomato juice (12 ounces)
³/₄ teaspoon black pepper
2 drops Tabasco or to taste
2 breadsticks (3 for 3 servings)

1. Dice the cucumber, tomato, and scallion into ¹/₄-inch pieces, or chop in a food processor.

2. Add the tomato juice, pepper, and Tabasco to the vegetables. Use Tabasco sparingly; start with 1 or 2 drops.

Serve with breadsticks.

For 2 servings
each serving contains

Calories	176	Fat	2g
Protein	7g	Cholesterol	1mg
Carbohydrates	37g	Sodium	236mg

For 3 servings
each serving contains

Calories	152	Fat	1g
Protein	5g	Cholesterol	1mg
Carbohydrates	31g	Sodium	225mg

Very Berry Yogurt Soup >

We've used this soup for entertaining, because it is not only extremely refreshing but pretty too. Most important, it is a wonderful source of vitamin C.

1/2 pint strawberries, hulled (green leaf cap removed) and sliced
1 cup orange juice
2 teaspoons lime juice
8 ounces plain low-fat yogurt
1 teaspoon honey
1/2 teaspoon cinnamon
1/2 teaspoon nutmeg
Fresh mint for garnish

1. Put half of the stawberries into a serving bowl. Put the other half into a blender. In the blender, add the orange juice, lime juice, yogurt, and honey. Blend on high until smooth. Add the cinnamon and nutmeg. Blend until well mixed.

2. Pour over the sliced berries.

3. Chill for one-half hour. Garnish with the fresh mint.

For 2 servings
each serving contains

Calories	160	Fat	1g
Protein	8g	Cholesterol	2mg
Carbohydrates	31g	Sodium	90mg

For 3 servings
each serving contains

Calories	107	Fat	<1g
Protein	5g	Cholesterol	1mg
Carbohydrates	21g	Sodium	60mg

Cucumber Vichyssoise ➤

Our version of this classic French soup increases the calcium and potassium at the expense of the fat. This is a great soup for a hot day. It also is a nice change from fruity yogurt recipes.

¹/₂ cup low-fat plain yogurt
1¹/₂ teaspoons dillweed
1¹/₂ teaspoons minced chives
1 medium cucumber
Salt and freshly ground black pepper to taste

1. Combine the yogurt, dillweed, and chives. Set aside.

2. Wash the cucumber, but do not peel it. Grate the cucumber into a bowl. Do not drain off any of the liquid.

3. Pour the yogurt mixture on the grated cucumber. Mix thoroughly.

4. Add salt and pepper to taste.

For 2 servings each serving contains				
Calories	84	Fat	<1g
Protein	7g	Cholesterol	2mg
Carbohydrates	13g	Sodium	90mg

For 3 servings each serving contains				
Calories	56	Fat	<1g
Protein	5g	Cholesterol	1mg
Carbohydrates	9g	Sodium	60mg

Rainbow Pepper Salad ➤

You can chase rainbows at any age, but chasing this one will add vitamin C and fiber to your high-performance diet. WARNING: If you are going to be drug-tested within two weeks, poppy seeds may cause a positive result.

1 medium red bell pepper
1 medium green bell pepper
1 medium yellow bell pepper
5¹/₂ ounces (¹/₂ can) mandarin oranges, drained
¹/₂ ounce enokitake mushrooms, cleaned and separated
2 tablespoons light mayonnaise
2 teaspoons balsamic vinegar
4 teaspoons sugar
2 teaspoons poppy seeds

1. Wash and remove the cores from all three peppers. Slice each pepper crossways into 4 pepper rings. Divide the pepper rings evenly among two or three serving plates, alternating the colors.

2. Place the mandarin oranges on top of the pepper rings. Place a few mushrooms over the mandarin oranges.

3. In a microwave-safe bowl, combine the mayonnaise, balsamic vinegar, and sugar. Mix the dressing until it is smooth. Microwave for 1 minute on high.

4. Add the poppy seeds to the dressing and mix thoroughly. Pour over the peppers.

For 2 servings	Calories	160	Fat	4g
each serving contains	Protein	2g	Cholesterol	0mg
	Carbohydrates	31g	Sodium	163mg

For 3 servings	Calories	107	Fat	3g
each serving contains	Protein	1g	Cholesterol	0mg
	Carbohydrates	21g	Sodium	109mg

Asian Mushroom Salad ➤

Americans have expanded their horizons from the white button mushroom to all sorts of exotic varieties. This recipe works well with any mushrooms; we chose these for variety, but you can substitute according to availability. This is an outstanding source of folic acid and vitamin K.

3 ounces raw fresh spinach
2 ounces fresh enokitake mushrooms
2 ounces fresh white button mushrooms
2 ounces fresh shiitake mushrooms
Nonstick vegetable spray
3 cloves garlic, minced
2 tablespoons balsamic vinegar
1 tablespoon soy sauce

1. Wash the spinach thoroughly and tear into small pieces. Clean and slice all the mushrooms.

2. Heat the pan on high for 30 seconds. Spray a nonstick skillet with nonstick vegetable spray. Add the garlic and all of the mushrooms. Immediately reduce the heat to low and cook the mushrooms until they begin to soften, about 7 minutes.

3. Combine the balsamic vinegar and soy sauce and mix into the mushrooms. Arrange the spinach on a plate and pour the mushrooms on top.

For 2 servings each serving contains	Calories	47	Fat	<1g
	Protein	4g	Cholesterol	0mg
	Carbohydrates	10g	Sodium	573mg

For 3 servings each serving contains	Calories	31	Fat	<1g
	Protein	2g	Cholesterol	0mg
	Carbohydrates	6g	Sodium	382mg

Red Coleslaw ➤

This is a nice change from classic coleslaw. One of the advantages of this version is that it is often easier to get a small amount of red cabbage, as opposed to green, at the grocery store. Red cabbage keeps well in the refrigerator; if kept in a lettuce crisper it can last for a month. So you don't need to use it all in one day. Cabbage and other cruciferous vegetables such as broccoli, cauliflower, and Brussels sprouts are believed to reduce the risk of cancer.

1 8-ounce can pineapple tidbits in their own natural juice
¹/₈ large or **¹/₂** small head red cabbage, shredded
2 tablespoons low-fat mayonnaise
1 tablespoon granulated sugar

1. Drain the pineapple into a bowl. Reserve the juice. Combine the cabbage with the pineapple.

2. Mix the juice, mayonnaise, and sugar in a bowl until the mixture is smooth and the sugar is dissolved.

3. Combine the dressing and the cabbage mixture. Blend until all the cabbage is lightly covered with dressing.

For 2 servings each serving contains				
	Calories	129	Fat	2g
	Protein	1g	Cholesterol	8mg
	Carbohydrates	29g	Sodium	22mg

For 3 servings each serving contains				
	Calories	86	Fat	1g
	Protein	<1g	Cholesterol	5mg
	Carbohydrates	19g	Sodium	15mg

Orange Carrot Salad ➤

I discovered this recipe in Israel. It is often served as part of a large breakfast before hard labor in the fields. It is an excellent source of the antioxidant vitamins A and C, as well as potassium. (KRFK)

2 medium carrots

1 tangarine, peeled and segmented (or use $^1/_2$ of an 11-ounce can of mandarin oranges, drained)

$^1/_4$ cup raisins

2 tablespoons honey

$^1/_8$ teaspoon cinnamon

$^1/_8$ teaspoon nutmeg

$^1/_4$ cup orange juice

1. Wash the carrots and shred them, using a carrot peeler or the shredder attachment on a food processor. Chop the tangerine into small pieces. Mix the carrots, tangerine, and raisins together.

2. Add the honey, cinnamon, and nutmeg. Toss the ingredients together until well mixed. Pour the orange juice over the carrot mixture. Chill until you are ready to serve.

For 2 servings
each serving contains

Calories	187	Fat	<1g
Protein	2g	Cholesterol	0mg
Carbohydrates	48g	Sodium	32mg

For 3 servings
each serving contains

Calories	125	Fat	<1g
Protein	1g	Cholesterol	0mg
Carbohydrates	32g	Sodium	21mg

Insalata Fresca ➤

The way food is presented is part of what makes for an appetizing meal that stimulates the hunger center of your brain. Take a few extra minutes to arrange these tasty and low-calorie ingredients into a pleasing pattern.

1 ripe red slicing tomato

2 ounces part-skim-milk mozzarella cheese

2 slices thinly sliced wheat bread, toasted and cut diagonally in half (we used Pepperidge Farm brand for the nutrient analysis; use 3 slices for 3 servings)

4 fresh basil leaves (6 leaves for 3 servings)

2 tablespoons balsamic vinegar

Freshly ground black pepper to taste

1. Slice the tomato and mozzarella thinly. Cut the cheese slices in half. Arrange the slices of tomato and cheese alternately on a plate, with the smaller slices of cheese placed on top of the tomato so that they can be seen. Use the toast points for decorating the plate.

2. Place fresh basil leaves in a decorative pattern between the slices. Sprinkle with the vinegar, and add black pepper to taste.

For 2 servings
each serving contains

Calories	160	Fat	5g
Protein	10g	Cholesterol	17mg
Carbohydrates	20g	Sodium	288mg

For 3 servings
each serving contains

Calories	125	Fat	4g
Protein	8g	Cholesterol	11mg
Carbohydrates	17g	Sodium	230mg

Nutty Fruit Salad ➤

This salad could be called the "anti-aging" salad. It is high in beta-carotene and vitamin C, and the almonds do their share to boost the vitamin E content. It's also refreshing as an after-workout snack. Any fresh, ripe, seasonal fruit can be used for this recipe. We chose these fruits for their variety of colors and flavors.

4 ripe strawberries, halved ($^1/_2$ cup)
$^1/_4$ cantaloupe melon, cubed (1 cup)
$^1/_4$ honeydew melon, cubed (1 cup)
$^1/_4$ cup blueberries
2 tablespoons slivered almonds

For the Honey-Yogurt Dressing

4 ounces plain nonfat yogurt
$^1/_8$ teaspoon vanilla
1$^1/_2$ tablespoons honey
1 fresh mint leaf, finely chopped

1. Prepare the fruit and mix it together gently with the almonds.

2. Blend all the dressing ingredients.

3. Serve the fruit with a dollop of Honey-Yogurt Dressing on the side, or with the dressing mixed into the fruit.

For 2 servings each serving contains	Calories	221	Fat	6g
	Protein	7g	Cholesterol	1mg
	Carbohydrates	39g	Sodium	62mg

For 3 servings each serving contains	Calories	147	Fat	4g
	Protein	5g	Cholesterol	<1mg
	Carbohydrates	26g	Sodium	41mg

Best of the Beef Salad ➤

My first experience eating this kind of salad was during a bike trip to Maine. Even though I was a vegetarian at the time, I politely ate the salad topped with beef served by a very gracious host for a luncheon on our way up the coast. It was a delightful surprise. I liked the taste of this beef, and it didn't weigh me down for the rest of the day's ride. (SMK)

¹/₂ pound filet mignon
1 clove garlic, minced
Freshly ground black pepper to taste
4 leaves red-tipped lettuce
4 leaves Boston lettuce
4 leaves endive
4 leaves escarole
4 mushrooms, sliced
¹/₂ large red pepper, julienned
7 ¹/₂ ounces canned white asparagus spears, drained
4 ounces cooked frozen peas
16 ounces frozen boiled whole potatoes, quartered
2 small whole-wheat pita breads (3 for 3 servings)
Olive oil cooking spray
Garlic powder
Onion powder
Heritage Dressing, 2 tablespoons per serving (recipe follows)
Freshly ground black pepper to taste

1. Rinse, dry, and season the filet with the fresh garlic and black pepper. Grill or broil the filet about 10 minutes on each side or until it is done to your liking (I prefer medium-well done, or very light brown in the center.)

2. While the beef is cooking, prepare the salad by washing, drying (or spinning), and tearing the greens and slicing the mushrooms and red pepper. Reheat the frozen peas and potatoes according to package directions. Place all the vegetables except the asparagus in a large salad bowl.

3. Thinly slice the cooked filets into 8 slices for 2 servings and 9 slices for 3 servings.

4. Lightly coat the pita bread with cooking spray and sprinkle with garlic powder and onion powder. Place under the broiler to toast for 2 minutes. Crumble the bread and sprinkle on the salad as croutons.

5. Put the salad on individual serving plates, decoratively top each with 4 slices of beef and half the white asparagus spears for 2 servings, or 3 slices of beef and ⅓ of the asparagus for 3 servings, and add 2 tablespoons of dressing to each serving. It is especially nice if the filet is still warm when served. Grind fresh pepper on the salad to taste.

For 2 servings
each serving contains

Calories	525	Fat	17g
Protein	38g	Cholesterol	72mg
Carbohydrates	58g	Sodium	752mg

For 3 servings
each serving contains

Calories	390	Fat	13g
Protein	26g	Cholesterol	48g
Carbohydrates	43g	Sodium	528mg

Heritage Dressing ➤

My Grandma Bessie was the originator of this recipe. Now all of the Kleiners have a version of their own. This recipe makes more salad dressing than you need for the Best of the Beef Salad. Use 2 tablespoons for each serving and refrigerate the rest for salad another day. (SMK)

3 tablespoons extra-virgin olive oil
¹/₄ cup red wine vinegar or balsamic vinegar
3 tablespoons water
1¹/₄ teaspoons garlic powder
¹/₈ teaspoon white pepper
¹/₂ teaspoon dried basil
¹/₂ teaspoon vegetable-seasoning salt (I like to use Vegesal)
1 tablespoon grated Parmesan cheese

1. Place all the ingredients in a jar with a lid. Shake well before serving.

   Makes ³/₄ cup, for 12 servings

Cool Cucumber Raita ➤

This traditional Indian dish is naturally high in calcium and is a wonderfully cool salad to serve alongside any spicy food that you like. It works well as a side dish to a hearty soup. It's even great to use as an appetizer dip. Just cut some whole-wheat pitas into triangles and toast them. Then do your bones some good and dip away.

¹/₂ English (seedless) cucumber
1 to **2** tablespoons finely chopped onion
8 ounces plain nonfat yogurt
¹/₈ teaspoon ground cumin
Dash cayenne pepper, or more to taste
2 teaspoons chopped fresh cilantro, or more to taste

1. Peel and coarsely grate the cucumber. Stir together with the onion and yogurt.

2. Heat the ground cumin for a few seconds in a small pan over medium heat to bring its flavor to life. Remove it from the heat and quickly stir in a little of the yogurt mixture. Return the yogurt-cumin mixture to the rest of the yogurt mixture and stir thoroughly.

3. Stir in the cayenne and chopped cilantro to taste. Serve chilled.

For 2 servings each serving contains				
Calories	82	Fat	0.5g
Protein	7g	Cholesterol	2mg
Carbohydrates	13g	Sodium	89mg

For 3 servings each serving contains				
Calories	55	Fat	<1g
Protein	5g	Cholesterol	1mg
Carbohydrates	9g	Sodium	59mg

Swimmer's Delight Pasta Salad ➤

This high-carbohydrate, high-powered pasta is a great carbohydrate-loading meal (see page 3) for the night before a race. Let it chill before serving. If you have leftovers, save them in the fridge overnight for lunch the next day. Purchase precooked shrimp in the deli section of your grocery, or use frozen, ready-to-cook shrimp that you cook at home. This salad travels well in a closed container that is kept chilled.

8 ounces dry whole-wheat or enriched pasta (shells, spirals, or elbows)
10-ounce package frozen mixed vegetables
8 ounces precooked popcorn shrimp or other small shrimp
1/2 cup Heritage Dressing (page 48)
1/4 cup (2 ounces) freshly grated Parmesan cheese
2 cups whole cherry tomatoes, halved

1. Cook the pasta according to package directions. Drain.

2. While the pasta cooks, heat the frozen vegetables according to package directions. Do not overcook. If you are cooking your own shrimp, do it at the same time as the vegetables.

3. Combine the cooked pasta, shrimp, and vegetables with Heritage Dressing. Mix well. Sprinkle on the cheese, and toss again.

4. Chill for about an hour. Add the tomatoes before serving.

For 2 servings each serving contains				
Calories	799	Fat	21g
Protein	51g	Cholesterol	230mg
Carbohydrates	112g	Sodium	558mg

For 3 servings each serving contains				
Calories	533	Fat	14g
Protein	34g	Cholesterol	153mg
Carbohydrates	74g	Sodium	372mg

Red-skinned Potato Salad ➤

My husband loves potato salad, but I hate peeling the potatoes. This is a wonderful compromise. It is also a wonderful source of potassium as well as vitamin C. (KRFK)

¹/₂ pound red-skinned potatoes (about 4 small or 2 large)
2 medium stalks celery, chopped
2 hard-boiled eggs, chopped
2 ounces low-fat mayonnaise
1 teaspoon prepared yellow mustard
¹/₂ teaspoon paprika
Salt and freshly ground black pepper to taste

1. Wash the potatoes, but do not peel them. Cut the potatoes into quarters and boil in water until they are soft but not mushy, about 15 minutes. When the potatoes are soft, put the pot in the sink and run cold water over the potatoes until they are cool. Drain.

2. Combine the potatoes with the celery and eggs.

3. Mix the mayonnaise, mustard, and paprika together. Coat the potato mixture with the mayonnaise mixture. Add salt and pepper to taste.

For 2 servings
each serving contains

Calories	289	Fat	11g
Protein	11g	Cholesterol	228mg
Carbohydrates	39g	Sodium	400mg

For 3 servings
each serving contains

Calories	193	Fat	7g
Protein	7g	Cholesterol	152mg
Carbohydrates	26g	Sodium	267mg

Chunky Cilantro Salsa ➤

My husband spent a few years living in Texas and developed a taste for very spicy food. This is his recipe for chunky salsa. If you like your food spicy, try this recipe. If you want a milder version, use half the amount of chili peppers. This recipe has chunks of vegetables you can toss into a food processor if you want a smoother sauce. If you purée the chili peppers, the distribution of the hot pepper oil will be increased and the dish will be spicier. This is a good source of vitamins A and C and magnesium. (KRFK)

1 medium tomato, diced
1 small onion, chopped
1/3 cucumber, unpeeled and chopped
1/4 cup chopped cilantro (10 sprigs)
2 small chilies, seeded and finely chopped
2 tablespoons lime juice
Salt and freshly ground black pepper to taste

1. Combine all the vegetables together and add the lime juice. Add the salt and pepper to taste.

For 2 servings
each serving contains

Calories	72	Fat	<1g
Protein	3g	Cholesterol	0mg
Carbohydrates	15g	Sodium	22mg

For 3 servings
each serving contains

Calories	48	Fat	<1g
Protein	2g	Cholesterol	0mg
Carbohydrates	10g	Sodium	15mg

Yogurt Cheese ➤

This recipe is included as a substitute for low-fat cream cheese, which is loaded with chemical additives. We use it in other recipes, but it can also be enjoyed plain on a bagel or spiced up with herbs or fruit. This recipe makes sixteen 1-tablespoon servings.

8 ounces plain nonfat yogurt
Cheesecloth or a yogurt cheese sieve

1. Pour the yogurt into the cheesecloth or sieve and place over a clean jar so that the liquid can drain from the solid without the solid touching the liquid. If using a cheesecloth, secure it to the jar with a rubber band. Refrigerate while draining. The longer you drain the yogurt, the firmer the cheese product (we recommend overnight).

2. Discard the liquid whey. Alternatively, you can save it; it is high in riboflavin and can be added to a soup or juice.

3. The yogurt cheese will remain fresh for up to two weeks if stored in a sealed container in the refrigerator. Other ingredients, such as herbs or fruit, can be added to the cheese to make unique flavors. This can shorten the shelf life.

For 16 servings
(1 tablespoon each)

each serving contains

Calories	7.5	Fat	. 0g
Protein	< 1g	Cholesterol	< 1mg
Carbohydrates	1g	Sodium	11mg

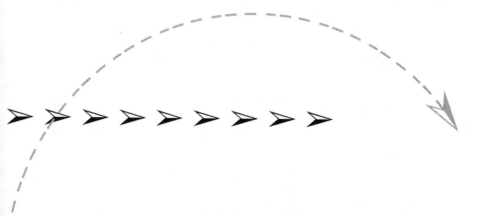

High-Test
FUELS
Pasta,
Potatoes,
and Rice

Vegetable Lasagna ➤

This is a simple variation on a classic Italian dish. The high-carbohydrate content is enhanced for the athlete by a significant reduction in fat.

4 whole-wheat lasagna noodles
Nonstick vegetable spray
1 small onion, chopped
1 15-ounce can tomato purée
1 6-ounce can tomato paste
1 teaspoon minced garlic
1 teaspoon dried oregano
1 teaspoon dried basil
8 ounces 1%-fat cottage cheese
8 ounces frozen broccoli, thawed
4 ounces shredded low-fat mozzarella

1. Preheat oven to 450°F. Cook the lasagna noodles according to package instructions. Meanwhile, heat a nonstick pan over medium heat, spray the nonstick frying pan with nonstick vegetable spray and sauté the onion until softened. Add the tomato purée, tomato paste, garlic, oregano, and basil to the pan. Stir to blend. Cook over low heat for 5 minutes.

2. Pour 1 tablespoon of the sauce into the bottom of an 8-inch × 4-inch loaf pan, or a standard size similar to this. Put in one layer of noodles followed by some of the cottage cheese, broccoli, tomato sauce, and a sprinkling of mozzarella. Add an additional layer of noodles and again add cottage cheese, broccoli, tomato sauce, and mozzarella. Finally, add a layer of noodles and cover with tomato sauce and a sprinkling of mozzarella.

3. Bake for 15 to 30 minutes or until bubbly and serve.

> ✳ **TIPS:** To lower the sodium content, use low-sodium cottage cheese. To thaw frozen vegetables quickly, run them under cold water.

For 2 servings each serving contains	Calories	626	Fat	13g
	Protein	45g	Cholesterol	37mg
	Carbohydrates	90g	Sodium	1,455mg

For 3 servings each serving contains	Calories	417	Fat	8g
	Protein	30g	Cholesterol	25mg
	Carbohydrates	60g	Sodium	970mg

Classic Macaroni ➤

This American classic has just been made better with its high-carbohydrate profile and low-fat body. A real beauty! If you object to American cheese, you can use a low-fat cheddar, but it will have a grainier consistency. This is a tasty way to add calcium to your diet.

6 ounces dry macaroni

Nonstick vegetable oil spray

2/3 cup skim milk

1 tablespoon cornstarch dissolved in ¹/₄ cup water

3 slices low-fat American cheese

¹/₄ teaspoon dry mustard

¹/₄ teaspoon freshly ground black pepper

1. Cook the macaroni in boiling water until tender, about 10 to 12 minutes.

2. Meanwhile, spray a nonstick pan with vegetable spray. Whisk the cornstarch mixture into the skim milk in the pan and heat on low until the milk begins to thicken. Crumble the cheese slices into the milk and continue stirring until melted. Add the dry mustard and pepper and mix thoroughly.

3. Drain the macaroni, toss with the sauce, and serve.

For 2 servings each serving contains	Calories	392	Fat	3g
	Protein	17g	Cholesterol	2mg
	Carbohydrates	72g	Sodium	220mg

For 3 servings each serving contains	Calories	261	Fat	2g
	Protein	11g	Cholesterol	1mg
	Carbohydrates	48g	Sodium	147mg

Whole-Wheat Pasta Treat ➤

This recipe is a great summer high-carbohydrate food. It's a terrific carbo-hydrate replacer, and since there is no mayonnaise, it will last a little bit longer in the heat than other salads. This dish is high in calcium, vitmain A, and niacin.

6 ounces tricolor whole-wheat (eggless) rotini

4 ounces frozen Oriental mixed vegetables or prepackaged fresh stir-fry vegetables

1 fresh tomato, seeded and chopped

¹/₄ cup fresh sliced mushrooms

1 tablespoon oregano

1 tablespoon basil

1 ounce grated Parmesan cheese

¹/₄ cup fat-free noncreamy Italian salad dressing

1. Cook the rotini in a large pot of boiling water until tender but not mushy, about 7 to 10 minutes.

2. Defrost the vegetables by cooking in the microwave, covered, for 3 minutes. If using fresh vegetables, steam them for the same length of time. Cool all of the cooked ingredients by running them under cold water.

3. Drain the pasta and cooked vegetables and place in a large bowl. Add remaining ingredients and toss together. Chill the salad until you are ready to serve it. It is best if chilled 1 hour or more, but it is fine to eat immediately.

For 2 servings each serving contains	Calories	528	Fat	8g
	Protein	24g	Cholesterol	20mg
	Carbohydrates	90g	Sodium	589mg

For 3 servings each serving contains	Calories	352	Fat	5g
	Protein	16g	Cholesterol	13mg
	Carbohydrates	60g	Sodium	393mg

Spinach Noodles with Hoisin Sauce ➤

This is a wonderful melding of the Orient with Italy—which means it is obviously an American hybrid. It is an excellent source of potassium (411 milligrams per serving, using the 2-serving portion size), which makes it a great electrolyte replacer.

6 ounces dried spinach noodles

1 teaspoon vegetable oil

¹/₂ cup sliced mushrooms

1 tablespoon minced garlic

2 ounces hoisin sauce (available in the Chinese section of most supermarkets)

1 cup water

2 scallions, diced

1. Bring a large pot of water to a boil. Add the spinach noodles and cook until tender, about 7 to 10 minutes.

2. While the water is boiling, heat the vegetable oil in a frying pan over medium heat. When the oil is hot, sauté the mushrooms and garlic. Add the hoisin sauce and continue to simmer. Add the water and combine well.

3. When the noodles are cooked, drain and toss them with the scallions and the sauce.

For 2 servings
each serving contains

Calories	448	Fat	6g
Protein	14g	Cholesterol	81mg
Carbohydrates	85g	Sodium	71mg

For 3 servings
each serving contains

Calories	298	Fat	4g
Protein	9g	Cholesterol	54mg
Carbohydrates	57g	Sodium	47mg

Pasta Porcini ➤

Pasta in Italy is more than noodles with sauce on top. This one-pot meal is based on the concept that if the pasta is cooked in the sauce, flavor will permeate the whole dish.

1 tablespoon flour

1/4 teaspoon freshly ground black pepper

1 teaspoon paprika

4 ounces fresh porcini mushrooms, cleaned and sliced

2 teaspoons unsalted butter

1 onion, diced

6 ounces dry pasta (shells or elbows work best)

2 cups water

1/2 medium zucchini, peeled, sliced, and julienned

1 large carrot, peeled, sliced, and julienned

1. Combine the flour, pepper, and paprika in a plastic bag. Shake the bag to mix. Toss the mushrooms into the bag and shake the bag to coat well.

2. Melt the butter in a nonstick pot over medium heat and sauté the diced onion and mushrooms for about five minutes, until they begin to soften. Add the dry pasta and water to the pot and cover it. Allow to simmer until almost all the water has been absorbed, about 10 to 15 minutes.

3. Toss the julienned zucchini and carrots on top of the pasta and cover the pot again. Cook until the remaining water has been absorbed, about 10 minutes.

For 2 servings each serving contains	Calories	420	Fat	6g
	Protein	14g	Cholesterol	10mg
	Carbohydrates	80g	Sodium	23mg

For 3 servings each serving contains	Calories	280	Fat	4g
	Protein	9g	Cholesterol	7mg
	Carbohydrates	53g	Sodium	15mg

Pasta Parmesan ➤

When you have had enough of tomato sauces, this nouvelle recipe will encourage you to eat yet another bowl of high-carbohydrate pasta.

6 ounces dry fettucini noodles
1 teaspoon unsalted butter
2 small onions, diced
1 cup sliced mushrooms
1 cup 2% milk
1 tablespoon cornstarch dissolved in ¹/₄ cup cold water
2 ounces grated Parmesan cheese
¹/₂ teaspoon freshly ground black pepper
1 ounce sherry
1 ounce sun-dried tomatoes, soaked in hot water for 5 minutes to soften, drain, then dice

1. Cook the fettucini in a pot of boiling water until it is tender.

2. Melt the butter in a frying pan over medium heat. Sauté the onions and mushrooms. Add the milk and the cornstarch mixture and whisk until blended. Continue whisking the sauce as it thickens, slowly adding the Parmesan cheese and pepper.

3. When the Parmesan cheese has melted, remove the pan from the heat and add the sherry, mixing it through the sauce. Toss the pasta, sauce, and tomatoes together.

For 2 servings each serving contains				
Calories	654	Fat	14g
Protein	31g	Cholesterol	37mg
Carbohydrates	95g	Sodium	613mg

For 3 servings each serving contains				
Calories	436	Fat	9g
Protein	21g	Cholesterol	24mg
Carbohydrates	63g	Sodium	408mg

Gnocchi in Caraway Sauce ➤

For an excellent but different-tasting carbohydrate load, try this recipe. It's based on a thick soup that my Grandma Rosie made. Its origins are in Marmorish, Hungary. This recipe smells like fresh rye bread. (KRFK)

2 tablespoons unsalted butter
4 tablespoons caraway seeds
2 tablespoons cornstarch dissolved in ¹/₄ cup cold water
9 ounces frozen or fresh gnocchi
3 cups water
Salt and freshly ground black pepper to taste

1. Melt the butter in a pot over low heat. Add the caraway seeds. Add the cornstarch mixture, gnocchi, and water. Bring to a boil and cook until the water is absorbed. You will have a creamy coating on the gnocchi. Add additional water if you want a thinner sauce.

2. Add salt and freshly ground black pepper to taste, and serve.

For 2 servings
each serving contains

Calories	540	Fat	16g
Protein	17g	Cholesterol	124mg
Carbohydrates	84g	Sodium	38mg

For 3 servings
each serving contains

Calories	360	Fat	11g
Protein	11g	Cholesterol	83mg
Carbohydrates	56g	Sodium	24mg

Champion Noodles ➤

This is a great replenishing meal to eat after a hot and heavy workout or race. It's high in carbohydrates to replace your used-up glycogen stores, and the extra sodium replaces the important electrolytes you lose when you sweat. The noodles taste best when they're cold.

1 1/2 tablespoons sesame oil
1 3/4 tablespoons soy sauce
3/4 tablespoon balsamic vinegar
1 tablespoon sugar
1/2 teaspoon salt
1/2 to 1 teaspoon chili oil, or to taste
1/2 pound fresh Chinese egg noodles or fettucini-style noodles
2 whole scallions, thinly sliced, plus more for garnish

1. Blend the sesame oil, soy sauce, balsamic vinegar, sugar, salt, and chili oil in a bowl.

2. Cook the noodles for 1 to 2 minutes, until tender but still firm. Drain, rinse two or three times in order to cool, and put in a large mixing bowl.

3. Pour the seasoning mixture over the noodles. Toss gently, then add the scallions and toss again. Put aside at room temperature for at least 30 minutes. It is best if left for an hour, or overnight in the refrigerator. To serve, toss again and garnish with more sliced scallions.

For 2 servings
each serving contains

Calories	576	Fat	16g
Protein	17g	Cholesterol	110mg
Carbohydrates	91g	Sodium	1,459mg

For 3 servings
each serving contains

Calories(25% Fat)	384	Fat	11g
Protein	11g	Cholesterol	73mg
Carbohydrates	60g	Sodium	972mg

Power Pasta ➤

These large portions make a great high-carbohydrate meal. To round it out, serve with a tossed salad. You can reduce the sodium content by using a low-sodium spaghetti sauce.

¹/₂ pound ground dark-meat turkey
¹/₂ teaspoon garlic powder
Pinch white pepper
12 ounces spaghetti sauce
¹/₂ pound whole-wheat spaghetti
¹/₄ cup freshly grated Parmesan cheese

1. Brown the meat in a nonstick saucepan over medium heat with the garlic powder and pepper. The meat should be thoroughly cooked. Add the sauce and cook until the sauce is heated.

2. Cook the pasta according to package directions. Pour the sauce over the pasta and sprinkle with Parmesan cheese.

For 2 servings
each serving contains

Calories	688	Fat	15g
Protein	31g	Cholesterol	31mg
Carbohydrates	116g	Sodium	1,147mg

For 3 servings
each serving contains

Calories	458	Fat	10g
Protein	21g	Cholesterol	20mg
Carbohydrates	77g	Sodium	765mg

Seashore Buckwheat ➤

This favorite family recipe reminds me of the sun and the shells at the shore. Buckwheat (or kasha) is a nutty-tasting grain that is a great source of carbohydrates and a good protein source. Refrigerate any leftovers and throw them into a cold green salad the next day for a nutty flavor. (SMK)

$^1/_3$ cup whole-wheat pasta shells (to yield $^1/_2$ cup cooked)
$^1/_2$ tablespoon canola oil
4 ounces mushrooms, sliced
$^1/_2$ small onion, diced
1 cup chicken stock
1 egg white, slightly beaten
$^1/_2$ cup preroasted buckwheat kernels or groats
Pinch white pepper

1. Cook the pasta shells until *al dente*, according to package directions, drain, and set aside.

2. Heat the oil in a nonstick pan over medium heat. Add the mushrooms and onion and sauté until the onion is translucent, about 5 to 7 minutes. Set aside.

3. Heat the stock to boiling. In a small mixing bowl, combine the egg white with the buckwheat until kernels are coated. Turn the buckwheat into a medium-size skillet and stir the egg and buckwheat mixture over medium-high heat for 3 to 4 minutes until it is hot and slightly toasted and the egg-coated kernels are well separated. Reduce the heat to low and carefully stir in the boiling stock, sautéed mushrooms and onions, and white pepper. Cover tightly and simmer 10 to 12 minutes, or until the buckwheat kernels are tender and all the liquid has been absorbed.

4. Turn into an oven-safe casserole dish and mix in the pasta shells. Place uncovered under an oven broiler for 3 to 5 minutes, just to brown the top. Watch closely and remove promptly.

For 2 servings each serving contains				
Calories	248	Fat	6g
Protein	10g	Cholesterol	0mg
Carbohydrates	43g	Sodium	395mg

For 3 servings each serving contains				
Calories	165	Fat	4g
Protein	6g	Cholesterol	0mg
Carbohydrates	27g	Sodium	263mg

Easy Energy Couscous ➤

There are many versions of this style of couscous. This recipe uses lots of dried fruits to boost the amounts of nutrients, especially carbohydrates, iron, and beta-carotene. Try to use whole-wheat couscous if you can find it.

2 tablespoons slivered almonds

2 tablespoons golden raisins

6 dried apricots, quartered

2 tablespoons dried figs, quartered

1/4 teaspoon cinnamon

1/4 cup fresh orange juice

3/4 cup water

1/4 teaspoon salt

1/2 tablespoon unsalted butter

1/2 cup couscous

1. Place the almonds, raisins, apricots, and figs in a bowl with the cinnamon. Cover with the orange juice and refrigerate for a minimum of 30 minutes, covered. It can marinate for as long as overnight.

2. In a saucepan bring the water, salt, and butter to a boil. Stir in the couscous, cover, and simmer over low heat for 5 minutes. Remove from heat and let stand 5 minutes. Fluff the couscous lightly with a fork.

3. Transfer the fruit-and-nut mixture to a saucepan and warm thoroughly over medium-low heat. Turn into a mixing bowl and add the cooked couscous. Mix well. Couscous can be served warm or cold.

For 2 servings
each serving contains

Calories	395	Fat	11g
Protein	10g	Cholesterol	8mg
Carbohydrates	67g	Sodium	309mg

For 3 servings
each serving contains

Calories	263	Fat	7g
Protein	7g	Cholesterol	5mg
Carbohydrates	45g	Sodium	206mg

✳ **ALTERNATIVE:** Substitute ¹/₂ cup freshly chopped apple for the apricots and figs.

First-Place Fries ➤

These fries are so fast and easy you won't believe it. And they're a first-rate, high-carbohydrate snack. Eat them hot out of the oven for the most crispness.

2 large white baking potatoes
1 medium onion, chopped
2 cloves garlic, minced
1 teaspoon paprika
1/2 teaspoon thyme
1/2 tablespoon freshly grated Parmesan cheese
1 tablespoon canola oil
1/4 cup water

1. Preheat oven to 450°F and place cooking rack at lowest setting. Cut the unpeeled, washed potatoes into julienne strips, as thin as possible (no more than ¼-inch thick).

2. Place the remaining ingredients in a blender or food processor and whirl for 20 seconds, until the onions are finely minced.

3. Place the potato strips on a nonstick cookie sheet. Spoon the onion-garlic mixture over the potatoes. Toss the potato strips in the mixture to coat (some of the mixture will not adhere to the potatoes).

4. Bake in the oven on bottom rack about 15 minutes. Turn the potatoes over. Bake 15 minutes more, until crisp and browned. Lift the potatoes off cookie sheet with a spatula. Serve hot.

For 2 servings
each serving contains

Calories	309	Fat	7g
Protein	6g	Cholesterol	1mg
Carbohydrates	56g	Sodium	42mg

For 3 servings
each serving contains

Calories	206	Fat	5g
Protein	4g	Cholesterol	<1mg
Carbohydrates	37g	Sodium	28mg

Praline Sweet Potatoes ➤
(or Anti-aging Power)

For a real taste of the South, this potato dish brings a new approach to a classic American favorite. Put it on your list for dishes high in beta-carotene, an important antioxidant.

1 large sweet potato, peeled and sliced into 1-inch rounds
¹/₄ cup water
1 cup fresh orange juice
¹/₂ cup brown sugar
2 teaspoons cornstarch dissolved in ¹/₄ cup cold water
¹/₄ cup chopped pecans
1 ounce bourbon (Amaretto can be substituted)
1 tablespoon butter

1. Place the potato slices and water in a shallow, microwave-safe dish with a lid. Microwave the potatoes on high for 7 to 10 minutes, or until soft.

2. While the potatoes are cooking, combine the orange juice, brown sugar, cornstarch mixture, and pecans in a small pot. Bring the sugar mixture to a boil, reduce the heat, and allow to simmer for 5 minutes. Add the bourbon and the butter. Heat until the butter is melted.

3. Drain the potatoes and pour the sauce over the potatoes, making sure all are coated. Place the potatoes back in the microwave and cook for 5 more minutes on high.

For 2 servings
each serving contains

Calories	558	Fat	15g
Protein	4g	Cholesterol	16mg
Carbohydrates	96g	Sodium	27mg

For 3 servings
each serving contains

Calories	372	Fat	10g
Protein	3g	Cholesterol	10mg
Carbohydrates	64g	Sodium	18mg

Baked Potato with Yogurt-Chive Sauce ➤

This old standby is jazzed up without a ton of fat. A classic baked potato would have 14 grams of fat and 365 calories. You get a 125-calorie savings. Add it to your carbohydrate-loading menu.

2 medium Idaho baking potatoes or 3 small potatoes

1/2 cup nonfat Yogurt Cheese (see page 53)

About **1** ounce sun-dried tomatoes, soaked in boiling water for 5 minutes to soften, then chopped

2 tablespoons chopped fresh chives

2 tablespoons toasted wheat germ

1. Wash and dry the potatoes. Place the potatoes in the microwave oven and cook on high until soft, approximately 8 minutes.

2. Meanwhile, combine the yogurt cheese, chopped sun-dried tomatoes, and chives.

3. When the potatoes are done, allow to rest for 3 minutes before cutting them in half. Add half the yogurt sauce to each potato for 2 servings or one-third the yogurt sauce for 3 servings, and top each with wheat germ.

For 2 servings
each serving contains

Calories	345	Fat	2g
Protein	14g	Cholesterol	1mg
Carbohydrates	70g	Sodium	61mg

For 3 servings
each serving contains

Calories	230	Fat	1g
Protein	9g	Cholesterol	<1mg
Carbohydrates	47g	Sodium	41mg

Caramelized Jerusalem Artichokes ➤

This unusual dish is similiar to potatoes, but with a sweet flavor. It can add variety to your everyday menu. For a non-meat dish, its iron content is relatively high at 3.8 milligrams per serving (using the 2-serving portion size).

1 teaspoon unsalted butter
1 small onion, sliced
8 ounces Jerusalem artichokes (or sunchokes), sliced
1 tablespoon paprika
1 ¹/₂ cups water

1. Melt the butter in a nonstick frying pan. Sauté the onion, artichokes, and paprika until the artichokes begin to brown.

2. Add the water and cover tightly until the water is absorbed and the artichokes are tender, about 20 minutes. If the artichokes are not tender when the water has been absorbed, add an additional ¹/₂ cup of water, cover, and continue cooking.

For 2 servings
each serving contains

Calories	128	Fat	3g
Protein	4g	Cholesterol	5mg
Carbohydrates	24g	Sodium	3mg

For 3 servings
each serving contains

Calories	85	Fat	2g
Protein	2g	Cholesterol	3mg
Carbohydrates	16g	Sodium	2mg

Brown Rice with Vegetables ➤

This fiber-packed casserole is a vegetarian's dream, but meat lovers love it too. It is a great source of beta-carotene for a high-antioxidant meal, as well as a good source of calcium.

1 cup (10-minute quick-cooking) brown rice
6 ounces frozen broccoli/cauliflower/red pepper mixture (or a mixture of your choice)
1 cup water
1 teaspoon rosemary
1 teaspoon sage
1/2 cup fat-free ricotta cheese
1 egg, beaten
2 ounces shredded part-skim-milk mozzarella

1. Combine the rice, vegetables, water, rosemary, and sage in a pot. Cover, bring to a boil, and then simmer until all the water is absorbed into the rice, about 10 minutes.

2. Fold in the ricotta cheese and the beaten egg until well blended. Place in a microwave-safe/oven-safe dish, and loosely cover. Cook the rice mixture in the microwave on high power for 5 minutes.

3. Sprinkle the mozzarella cheese on top and continue heating until the cheese melts, or place under the broiler for 2 minutes. Serve immediately.

For 2 servings each serving contains				
Calories	530	Fat	10g
Protein	29g	Cholesterol	132mg
Carbohydrates	83g	Sodium	297mg

For 3 servings each serving contains				
Calories	353	Fat	7g
Protein	19g	Cholesterol	88mg
Carbohydrates	55g	Sodium	198mg

Rice and Vermicelli ➤

This pasta-and-rice combination gives additional variety to your menu and is an easy one-pot carbohydrate load. It makes a great electrolyte replacer if the chicken stock used isn't the low-sodium version.

1 tablespoon unsalted butter
1 cup (10-minute quick-cooking) brown rice
2 ounces dry spaghetti (broken into 1-inch pieces)
1 cup low-sodium chicken stock
1 cup hot water
1 tablespoon dried parsley flakes

1. Melt the butter in a nonstick frying pan that has a lid. Add the rice and spaghetti and sauté until light brown. Add the chicken stock and water. Add the parsley and cover the pan.

2. Reduce the heat to low and cook until all the water has been absorbed, approximately 10 minutes.

For 2 servings
each serving contains

Calories	527	Fat	9g
Protein	12g	Cholesterol	17mg
Carbohydrates	98g	Sodium	413mg

For 3 servings
each serving contains

Calories	351	Fat	6g
Protein	8g	Cholesterol	11mg
Carbohydrates	65g	Sodium	275mg

Fried Rice ➤

Fried rice can be a wonderful side dish or main course in a classic Chinese meal. You can easily toss in a small amount of an already-cooked meat or seafood, such as shrimp, if you want to add protein.

1 tablespoon soy sauce
¹/₄ teaspoon sugar
¹/₂ teaspoon cooking sherry
2 tablespoons vegetable oil
2 tablespoons chopped scallions
1 cup frozen peas and carrots, thawed
2 cups cooked white rice (instant is fine, or use leftovers)
2 eggs, beaten

1. Combine the soy sauce, sugar, and sherry and set aside.

2. Heat the oil in a large pan or wok over high heat. Add the scallions and peas and carrots and cook until heated. Add the rice and fold into the vegetables.

3. Add the soy sauce mixture to the rice, blending thoroughly. Fold in the beaten eggs and mix through the rice. Continue cooking until the eggs are firm. Serve immediately.

For 2 servings
each serving contains

Calories	417	Fat	13g
Protein	15g	Cholesterol	213mg
Carbohydrates	61g	Sodium	637mg

For 3 servings
each serving contains

Calories	278	Fat	9g
Protein	10g	Cholesterol	142mg
Carbohydrates	41g	Sodium	425mg

Sumptuous Stuffing ➤

Stuffing is a traditional dish in many families. This recipe is a new and healthful alternative to an old favorite.

1 tablespoon unsalted butter
1 1/2 small onions, chopped
1/3 cup chopped mushrooms
1 stalk celery, chopped
1 tablespoon chopped fresh parsley
5 slices fat-free bread, toasted
1/8 teaspoon freshly ground black pepper
2/3 cup low-sodium chicken stock
2 egg whites

1. Melt the butter in a nonstick pan over medium heat. Sauté the onions, mushrooms, celery, and parsley until soft, about 5 minutes. Remove from the heat.

2. Cut the toasted bread into croutons. Combine the croutons with the vegetables and mix lightly. Pour the broth over the croutons and toss lightly. Beat the egg whites and stir into the crouton mixture.

3. Spoon the stuffing into a microwave-safe casserole and cover it loosely. Microwave the stuffing on high power for 5 to 7 minutes (use the longer time for lower-wattage microwaves). Let the stuffing remain covered for an additional 3 minutes to finish cooking. If you prefer baked stuffing, place in an oven-safe dish and bake at 450°F for 30 minutes.

For 2 servings
each serving contains

Calories	235	Fat	8g
Protein	12g	Cholesterol	17mg
Carbohydrates	27g	Sodium	648mg

For 3 servings
each serving contains

Calories	157	Fat	5g
Protein	8g	Cholesterol	11mg
Carbohydrates	18g	Sodium	432mg

5

Vegetarian VIGOR Vegetable Entrées and Sides

Burrito Magnifico ➤

When I first became a vegetarian, this was one of my favorite dishes. It was easy to make, it was cheap, and even my dad liked it. Now we know that beans help prevent heart disease, and it is still one of my favorites. I prefer black beans to pinto beans, but the choice is yours. (Note: The nonfat cheese adds most of the sodium. Using part-skim-milk mozzarella will lower the sodium but slightly increase the fat.) (SMK)

1 cup (8 ounces) canned pinto or black beans
2 flour tortillas (3 for 3 servings)
1/2 cup shredded nonfat mozzarella
4 lettuce leaves, shredded
2 small tomatoes, chopped
1 cup (8 ounces) salsa (you can use the recipe in the "Soups and Salads" section, page 52, or simply buy a ready-made version)
1/4 cup light sour cream

1. Place the beans in a microwave-safe dish and heat in microwave oven on high for 1½ minutes (or cook for 3 minutes in a saucepan over medium heat).

2. Meanwhile, heat a large frying pan over medium heat. Place a tortilla in the pan and warm for 1 to 2 minutes, turning once. Remove the tortilla to a plate when warm and very slightly browned.

3. Place ½ cup of beans in center of the tortilla. Cover with half of the cheese, lettuce, and tomatoes. Roll tortilla closed and place the folded side down on a serving plate.

4. Pour half of the salsa over the tortilla and top with 1 tablespoon of sour cream. Repeat with the rest of the tortillas.

For 2 servings each serving contains	Calories	600	Fat	8g
	Protein	37g	Cholesterol	10mg
	Carbohydrates	99g	Sodium	1,900mg

For 3 servings each serving contains	Calories	487	Fat	7g
	Protein	27g	Cholesterol	7mg
	Carbohydrates	81g	Sodium	1,430mg

Spinach Cheese Burrito ➤

A burrito is a filled flour tortilla. This version uses cheese and vegetables, but any filling can be used. The cheese and spinach mixture is an excellent source of calcium, with 400 milligrams per serving. This recipe proves that Mexican food can be light and low in fat as well as flavorful.

Nonstick vegetable spray
1/2 small onion, chopped
1/2 stalk celery, chopped
1/4 bell pepper, chopped
10-ounce package frozen chopped spinach, thawed and drained
3 cloves garlic, minced
1 cup dry-curd cottage cheese
Salt and freshly ground black pepper to taste
2 flour tortillas (3 for 3 servings)
1/8 cup salsa (you can use the recipe in the "Soups and Salads" section, page 52, or simply buy a ready-made version)
1/8 cup shredded jack cheese

1. Spray a nonstick pan with nonstick vegetable spray. Sauté the onion, celery, bell pepper, spinach, and garlic together over medium-high heat until the vegetables are tender, about 10 minutes. Drain well.

2. Mash the cottage cheese curds with a fork until they are broken up into small pieces. Add the vegetables, salt, and pepper to the cottage cheese and mix thoroughly.

3. Spoon some of the mixture onto one end of each tortilla. Roll the tortillas into tubes and place in a square baking pan. Cover the pan and bake at 400°F for 10 minutes. Uncover the pan, put the salsa and shredded cheese on top of the tortillas, and cook an additional 5 minutes. Serve hot.

For 2 servings each serving contains				
Calories	319	Fat	7g
Protein	26g	Cholesterol	20mg
Carbohydrates	38g	Sodium	522mg

For 3 servings each serving contains				
Calories	191	Fat	5g
Protein	18g	Cholesterol	13mg
Carbohydrates	22g	Sodium	347mg

Tasty Tostadas ➤

A tostada is traditionally served like a layered salad, with the tortilla on the bottom. It makes a great weekend lunch or dinner (make extra for lunch the next day), and the beans will help to control your cholesterol and blood-sugar levels. The recipe can be made in a toaster oven.

1 cup (8 ounces) canned pinto or black beans
4 corn tortillas (for 3 servings, use 6 corn tortillas)
1/2 cup shredded nonfat cheddar cheese
2/3 small onion, chopped
1 small tomato, chopped
2/3 green pepper, chopped
1/4 cup light sour cream
4 large lettuce leaves, shredded
Salsa

1. Preheat oven to 450°F. Warm the beans in a saucepan over medium heat, or in microwave on high for 1 minute.

2. Spread each tortilla with beans, then sprinkle each with ¼ of the cheese. Heat the tortilla in preheated oven, or in toaster oven at 400°F, until the cheese melts.

3. Sprinkle with onion, tomato, and pepper. Spread with sour cream and top with lettuce and salsa.

For 2 servings each serving contains	Calories	337	Fat	5g
	Protein	24g	Cholesterol	10mg
	Carbohydrates	55g	Sodium	818mg

For 3 servings each serving contains	Calories	268	Fat	4g
	Protein	17g	Cholesterol	7mg
	Carbohydrates	45g	Sodium	546mg

Frijoles Vivido ➤

As scientists discover more about the disease-preventing qualities of beans, we've been including them in our diets more frequently. This filling recipe is a great carbohydrate-loading meal. A new product called Beano, available at most drugstores and natural-food stores, is an enzyme that will help your digestive tract with the troublesome aspects of eating beans.

1 teaspoon canola oil
2 cloves garlic, minced
1 small onion, chopped
¹/₂ sweet green pepper, chopped
¹/₄ pound Canadian bacon, chopped
¹/₂ cup enriched white rice
1 cup water
2 cups canned black beans
¹/₈ teaspoon freshly ground black pepper
1 tablespoon chopped fresh parsley (about 3 sprigs)
1 or **2** drops Tabasco sauce, or to taste
¹/₄ cup finely chopped sweet red pepper (½ medium pepper)
¹/₄ cup frozen sweet corn

1. Heat a nonstick skillet with the oil on medium-high for 45 seconds. Add the garlic and heat for another 30 to 40 seconds. Add the onion, green pepper, and Canadian bacon and sauté for 7 minutes, or until the vegetables are soft.

2. Meanwhile, begin cooking the rice in the 1 cup water according to package directions.

3. Add the beans, black pepper, parsley, and Tabasco to the onion mixture, lower the heat to low, cover, and cook until rice is done, about 15 to 20 minutes, stirring occasionally.

4. Rinse the frozen corn in a sieve or colander under warm water for 30 seconds. Just as the rice is done cooking, open the cover and quickly add corn and red pepper to the top of the rice. Close the cover at once; do not mix the vegetables into the rice. Let sit, covered, for 5 minutes. Fluff the corn and pepper into the rice.

5. Transfer the rice to a serving platter. Spoon the beans over the rice, allowing a ring of rice to show out from under the edge of the beans.

For 2 servings	Calories	556	Fat	8g
each serving contains	Protein	31g	Cholesterol	28mg
	Carbohydrates	92g	Sodium	1,727mg

For 3 servings	Calories	371	Fat	5g
each serving contains	Protein	21g	Cholesterol	19mg
	Carbohydrates	61g	Sodium	1,151mg

Tortellini in Brodo with Artichokes ➤

Serving tortellini in broth rather than in a heavy sauce keeps the cheese filling from being overpowered. This dish is an excellent electrolyte-replenisher as well as a good source of vitamin A.

10 sun-dried tomatoes (1 ounce), chopped

1 cup boiling water

1 teaspoon olive oil

1 clove garlic, minced

14-ounce can artichoke hearts in brine, drained and chopped

1 cup fresh basil, chopped

1¹/₂ cups chicken broth

9 ounces refrigerated cheese tortellini, cooked

1 tablespoon chopped fresh parsley (a couple of sprigs)

1 tablespoon Parmesan cheese

1. Soak the sun-dried tomatoes in boiling water for 5 minutes. Drain.

2. Heat the olive oil on medium until hot. Sauté the garlic, sun-dried tomatoes, artichokes, and basil for 5 minutes. Add the broth and simmer for 10 minutes on low.

3. Add the tortellini to the sauce and coat the pieces by tossing lightly. Place on a platter and garnish with the parsley and Parmesan cheese.

For 2 servings	Calories	590	Fat	14g
each serving contains	Protein	35g	Cholesterol	71mg
	Carbohydrates	81g	Sodium	2,000mg

For 3 servings	Calories	393	Fat	9g
each serving contains	Protein	23g	Cholesterol	47mg
	Carbohydrates	54g	Sodium	1,333mg

The **High Performance** Cookbook

Grilled Hawaiian Tofu ➤

This is a beautiful entrée that takes hardly any time to prepare. Add brown rice and a tossed salad to round out the meal. The plantain is a great source of vitamin B-6. If you can't find plantain, skip it and serve just the pineapple rings on top of the tofu. The recipe works best on a grill.

3 tablespoons balsamic vinegar

1 tablespoon soy sauce

2 tablespoons peanut oil

1 teaspoon fresh minced ginger

2 cloves garlic, minced

1 pound fresh tofu

1 plantain

15-ounce can pineapple rings in natural juice

1 tablespoon brown sugar

1. For the marinade, mix together the vinegar, soy sauce, peanut oil, ginger, and garlic.

2. Slice tofu into ½-inch-thick slices and marinate for about 20 minutes, but no longer than 30 minutes. Brush most of the marinade off the tofu and place tofu on heated grill. Grill for 10 minutes, turning once after 5 minutes.

3. Peel and slice the plantain in half and then lengthwise into 8 slices. Sprinkle the plantain and pineapple slices lightly with brown sugar and place on grill during the last 3–4 minutes of cooking. Watch closely so the sugar browns but doesn't burn.

4. Serve by layering tofu, pineapple, and plantain, in that order.

✳ **NOTE:** If the tofu is soft and might slide through the rungs of the grill top, it is helpful to use a slotted pan or hole-punched pan to cook the tofu on top of the grill. These pans are usually sold as a helpful tool for grilling fish. A broiler-pan insert will also work.

For 2 servings	Calories	469	Fat	12g
each serving contains	Protein	18g	Cholesterol	0mg
	Carbohydrates	81g	Sodium	153mg

For 3 servings	Calories	313	Fat	8g
each serving contains	Protein	12g	Cholesterol	0mg
	Carbohydrates	54g	Sodium	102mg

Tofu Spaghetti ➤

This should be a staple recipe in your diet. It's high in carbohydrates and low in fat, with a good amount of protein. We eat this once a week at least. It's a real belly-filler.

Nonstick cooking spray
1/2 pound crumbled tofu
4 fresh mushrooms, sliced (½ cup)
1 medium green pepper, diced (½ cup)
1 small onion, diced (¼ cup)
16 ounces Homemade Marinara Sauce (recipe follows)
1/2 pound dry whole-wheat noodles

1. Bring a large pot of water to a boil over medium heat.

2. Meanwhile, lightly coat a nonstick frying pan with cooking spray. Add the tofu and cook over medium-high heat for 5 minutes. Add the mushrooms, pepper, and onion and cook until tender, about 7 to 10 minutes.

3. Add the spaghetti sauce, cover, and simmer over low heat for 10 minutes.

4. While the sauce is cooking, cook the noodles according to package directions. Drain. Serve the sauce over the noodles.

For 2 servings	Calories	607	Fat	9g
each serving contains	Protein	29g	Cholesterol	0mg
	Carbohydrates	115g	Sodium	197mg

For 3 servings	Calories	405	Fat	6g
each serving contains	Protein	20g	Cholesterol	0mg
	Carbohydrates	77g	Sodium	131mg

The **High Performance** Cookbook

Homemade Marinara Sauce

1 teaspoon olive oil

1 clove garlic, minced

2 ounces red wine

28-ounce can no-salt crushed tomatoes in purée

6-ounce can no-salt tomato paste

4 ounces tomato sauce

1 cup water

¹/₄ teaspoon oregano

¹/₄ teaspoon dried basil

¹/₈ teaspoon pepper

1. Sauté the garlic in the olive oil for 1 minute. Add the wine and cook for 2 more minutes. Add all other ingredients and mix thoroughly. Cover and bring to a boil, then reduce heat and simmer for 30 minutes.

✳ **OPTIONAL** Sauté chopped onions, mushrooms, and/or green peppers with the garlic, oil, and wine.

Makes approximately five 1-cup servings. You can freeze any leftover sauce.

Each 1-cup
serving contains

Calories	102	Fat	2g
Protein	4g	Cholesterol	0mg
Carbohydrates	22g	Sodium	178mg

PASTA SAUCES

Ready-to-eat pasta sauces are generally very high in sodium. For those of you who don't have the time to make your own marinara, here's a list of our favorite pasta sauces that are available nationally, along with their nutritional information. You might find local brands that you like just as much. Healthful brands have no more than 2 grams of fat per serving. Note that the serving size is ½ cup, and we suggest a 1-cup serving of sauce to cover a hefty plate of high-carbohydrate pasta.

BRAND	SVG. SIZE (oz.)	CALORIES	FAT (g)	SODIUM (mg)
Contadina				
Light Chunky Tomato	5	50	0	570
Light Garden Veg.	5	50	0	620
Healthy Choice				
Chunky Italian	4	40	0	350
Garlic & Herbs	4	40	<1	350
Meat	4	50	<1 (2 mg cholesterol)	380
Mushrooms	4	40	<1	390
Traditional	4	40	<1	350
Newman's Own				
Bandito Diavolo	4	70	2	530
Sockarooni	4	70	2	560
Venetian Style	4	70	2	560
Venetian Style w/ Mushrooms	4	70	2	560

Traveling Noodle Veggie Casserole ➤

This is a recipe that I've been giving to athletes for years. It makes a great dinner to eat at home. It also travels well if kept cool, and it can be reheated in no time if you are on the go. To lower the sodium content, use low-sodium soy sauce and part-skim-milk mozzarella (which will add fat to the recipe). (SMK)

4 ounces flat whole-wheat noodles
Nonstick cooking spray
1 teaspoon minced ginger
1 clove garlic, minced
1/2 pound tofu, cubed
1/2 small yellow summer squash, thinly sliced
1/2 small zucchini, thinly sliced
1 medium onion, sliced
4 fresh mushrooms, sliced
1 teaspoon soy sauce
1 egg white
1/2 cup shredded nonfat mozzarella
1/4 cup grated Parmesan

1. Preheat oven to 350°F. Boil the noodles according to package directions.

2. While the noodles are cooking, heat a large nonstick frying pan (a wok or wok-style pan is the best) for 30 seconds over medium-high heat. Spray pan with nonstick cooking spray. Cook the ginger and garlic first, for about 40 seconds. Quickly add the tofu, yellow squash, zucchini, onion, and mushrooms (in that order) and lightly stir-fry for 5 minutes. Add the soy sauce and stir-fry for 2 more minutes. Turn off heat but leave the vegetables in the pan.

3. When the noodles are done, drain them thoroughly and add to the cooked vegetables while the noodles and vegetables are still hot. Mix with a plastic or wooden spoon or spatula. Add the egg white and mozzarella and mix again.

4. Turn the mixture into a 1-quart oven-safe casserole dish, sprinkle Parmesan on top, and place uncovered in preheated oven for 15 minutes. To brown the Parmesan cheese topping, turn on broiler for the last 1 to 2 minutes of cooking. Watch closely so cheese browns but does not burn.

For 2 servings	Calories	410	Fat	8g
each serving contains	Protein	33g	Cholesterol	13mg
	Carbohydrates	56g	Sodium	600mg

For 3 servings	Calories	273	Fat	5g
each serving contains	Protein	22g	Cholesterol	9mg
	Carbohydrates	38g	Sodium	400mg

Sunshine Veggie Egg Salad ➤

My inspiration for this recipe came when I had run out of ideas for vegetarian sandwiches to brown-bag to college. I didn't have nonfat mayo back then, so I used homemade skim-milk yogurt instead. This recipe is much better. (SMK)

¹/₂ pound fresh tofu (not the kind in the box; it's higher in fat)
1¹/₂ tablespoons nonfat mayonnaise
¹/₂ tablespoon Dijon mustard
Pinch salt
Pinch white pepper
¹/₂ teaspoon dillweed
¹/₂ tablespoon sunflower seeds
1 teaspoon sweet pickle relish
4 slices fresh rye bread (6 slices for 3 servings)

1. Squeeze out any extra water in the tofu by pressing it in a paper towel. Mash the tofu with a fork or potato masher. Add all the remaining ingredients except the bread and mix well.

2. Spread half of the mixture on each of 2 bread slices; top with remaining bread to make 2 sandwiches.

For 2 servings	Calories	236	Fat	7g
each serving contains	Protein	14g	Cholesterol	<1mg
	Carbohydrates	33g	Sodium	568mg

For 3 servings	Calories	198	Fat	5g
each serving contains	Protein	11g	Cholesterol	<1mg
	Carbohydrates	31g	Sodium	472mg

Baba Ganouj ➤

My first encounter with baba ganouj was in Cairo, Egypt. I couldn't believe that this dish was really made with eggplant. Unfortunately the authentic dish is much higher in fat, but our recipe is a winning substitute. This spreadable dish travels well, so it's great for lunch on a day hike in the woods. It makes a great appetizer, as well as a meal. This recipe yields extra sesame sauce, which can be refrigerated and used in a second recipe or eaten as a dip. (SMK)

1 pound eggplant
¹/₄ cup Sesame Sauce (recipe follows)
¹/₃ cup fresh lemon juice
¹/₂ teaspoon salt
¹/₈ teaspoon white pepper
¹/₄ teaspoon olive oil
Pinch cayenne pepper
2 tablespoons chopped fresh cilantro or parsley
2 whole-wheat pita breads (3 for 3 servings)

1. Prick the eggplant with a fork in several places and cook in the microwave on high for 10 minutes, or until it is soft throughout. Cut the cooked eggplant in half and let it sit until cool enough to handle. Scrape out all the pulp from the skin and discard the skin.

2. Put the pulp into the bowl of a food processor. Add the sesame sauce, lemon juice, salt, and white pepper and process until the eggplant is minced and the mixture is slightly smooth.

3. Spread the eggplant mixture evenly in a shallow serving dish. Drizzle with olive oil and sprinkle with cayenne pepper and chopped cilantro or parsley. Chill before serving. Eat by using the pita bread to scoop up the baba ganouj.

For 2 servings each serving contains	Calories	293	Fat	10g
	Protein	10g	Cholesterol	0mg
	Carbohydrates	45g	Sodium	898mg

For 3 servings each serving contains	Calories	250	Fat	7g
	Protein	9g	Cholesterol	0mg
	Carbohydrates	41g	Sodium	712mg

Sesame Sauce

1/4 cup tahini (sesame seed paste)
1 large clove garlic, crushed or finely minced
2 tablespoons fresh lemon juice
2 tablespoons cold water

1. Stir the tahini and garlic together in a deep bowl. Beat in the lemon juice and water. The sauce should be slightly thick, not runny. If it is too thick, beat in a little more water.

Makes ¼ cup

Jerusalem Hummus ➤

We can't say enough about beans. They're high in fiber and carbohydrate, low in fat, and are a great source of plant protein. This vegetarian dish travels well, especially in a backpack. Make the hummus and cut the veggies at home. Take them in separate containers, and don't stuff the pita for a sandwich until you are ready to eat. Leftovers will be great for a few days.

1 cup (8 ounces) canned chickpeas
1 tablespoon plus 1 teaspoon lemon juice
1 small clove garlic
1 tablespoon tahini (sesame paste)
1/2 teaspoon chopped fresh parsley
Salt and freshly ground black pepper to taste
2 whole-wheat pita breads (3 for 3 servings)
1 green pepper, cut into thin rings
1/2 small onion, cut into thin slices
1 small tomato, thinly sliced
Handful of alfalfa sprouts

1. Drain the chickpeas, saving 2 tablespoons of the liquid. In a blender or food processor, mix the chickpeas and canned liquid, lemon juice, garlic, tahini, parsley, salt, and pepper. Blend until smooth (this may take several minutes). Hummus can also be made by mashing chickpeas with a fork or potato masher.

2. Warm the pitas in an oven or toaster. Cut in half and stuff each pita half with some of the prepared vegetables and a couple of tablespoons of hummus.

For 2 servings each serving contains	Calories	393	Fat	7g
	Protein	15g	Cholesterol	0mg
	Carbohydrates	70g	Sodium	834mg

For 3 servings each serving contains	Calories	317	Fat	5g
	Protein	12g	Cholesterol	0mg
	Carbohydrates	58g	Sodium	669mg

Autumn in the Smokies ➤

This savory recipe is a reminder of the spectacular autumn foliage in the Great Smoky Mountains of North Carolina. Its high beta-carotene content makes it an antioxidant dream.

1 whole acorn squash (1½ squashes for 3 servings)
¹/₂ cup long-grain brown rice
1 cup water
Nonstick cooking spray
4 fresh mushrooms, sliced
1 medium onion, diced
²/₃ pound tofu, cut into very small cubes (1 cup)
¹/₄ cup unsalted sunflower seeds
¹/₄ teaspoon sage
¹/₄ teaspoon marjoram
¹/₄ teaspoon thyme
1 teaspoon soy sauce
¹/₄ cup water

1. Cut the squash in half lengthwise and scoop out the seeds and stringy portion. Place cut side down in microwave-safe dish. Fill dish with ¼ inch of water. Cover with microwave-safe plastic wrap, leaving one corner unsealed. Cook in the microwave on high for 10 minutes, or until the squash is tender throughout.

2. Meanwhile, toast the rice in a nonstick frying pan over medium-high heat for 3 to 4 minutes until browned. In a saucepan, bring the 1 cup water to a boil and add it carefully to the toasted rice. Cover and cook over low heat until the rice is tender and the water is completely absorbed, about 15 to 20 minutes.

3. Place a nonstick frying pan over medium heat. Coat with nonstick cooking spray. Add the mushrooms and onion and cook, stirring, for a few minutes, until the onion is translucent. Add the tofu and sunflower seeds, stir, and cook 1 minute more. Add the herbs and soy sauce, stir again, and add the ¼ cup water.

4. Reduce heat to low and simmer uncovered for 5 to 10 minutes, stirring occasionally, until liquid is almost gone. Add the cooked rice, mixing together well, and cook a few minutes more.

5. Fill and surround each cooked squash half with some of the stuffing, and serve.

For 2 servings each serving contains	Calories	480	Fat	14g
	Protein	18g	Cholesterol	0mg
	Carbohydrates	78g	Sodium	196mg

For 3 servings each serving contains	Calories	358	Fat	9g
	Protein	13g	Cholesterol	0mg
	Carbohydrates	62g	Sodium	132mg

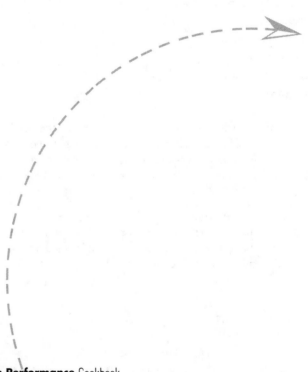

Acorn Squash with Apples ➤

Squash is indigenous to the United States and has been a staple of native American cuisine for centuries. This simple, sweet recipe is bursting with beta-carotene and will become a staple in your diet too.

1 medium acorn squash
1 large apple, diced
¹/₄ cup brown sugar
2 teaspoons cinnamon
1 teaspoon nutmeg
1 tablespoon unsalted butter

1. Pierce the acorn squash with a sharp knife in 4 or 5 places. Put the squash on the floor of the microwave oven on top of several layers of paper towel. Microwave on high for 5 minutes. (To cook the squash conventionally, cut it in half, remove seeds, and place in a pan, cut side down, with ½ inch of water. Bake the squash at 375°F for 35 to 40 minutes.)

2. While the squash is cooking, combine the apple with the brown sugar, cinnamon, and nutmeg. Cut the butter into small pieces and combine with the apple mixture.

3. Turn the squash over and microwave for an additional 5 minutes. Carefully remove the squash from the microwave and cut it in two identical halves. (Remember, it's hot!) Remove the seeds with a spoon.

4. Place the acorn squash in a microwave-safe dish, cut side up. Spoon half of the apple mixture into each cavity of the acorn squash. Microwave for 3 minutes on high. Remove from the microwave and serve.

For 2 servings each serving contains	Calories	426	Fat	7g
	Protein	10g	Cholesterol	0mg
	Carbohydrates	89g	Sodium	6mg

For 3 servings each serving contains	Calories	284	Fat	5g
	Protein	7g	Cholesterol	0mg
	Carbohydrates	59g	Sodium	4mg

Savory Squash Squares ➤

Say its name three times fast, and then enjoy this quick meal. The fragrant squash casserole can be eaten as a full meal or as a side dish. It provides an excellent protein:carbohydrate:fat ratio and is a good electrolyte replenisher.

1 medium butternut squash
2 ounces mushrooms, chopped
2 small onions, chopped
10 sprigs fresh parsley, chopped
1 clove garlic, minced
1/2 teaspoon oregano
1/2 teaspoon basil
1/2 14-ounce can (1 cup) peeled chopped tomatoes
1 cup 1%-fat cottage cheese
Nonstick vegetable spray
1/4 cup bulgur wheat

1. Prick the outside of the squash with a sharp knife and place on the floor of the microwave oven on several layers of paper towel. Microwave on high for 10 minutes. (To cook the squash conventionally, cut it in half and remove the seeds. Bake it, cut side down, in ½ inch of water at 375°F for 35 to 40 minutes.)

2. While the squash is cooking, sauté the mushrooms, onions, parsley, garlic, oregano, and basil together over medium heat until tender, for about 10 minutes. Add the tomatoes and continue cooking for 3 minutes. Remove from the heat and add the cottage cheese.

3. Peel and seed the squash (remember, it's hot, and you don't need to seed it if you cooked it conventionally and did so earlier). Cut the squash into 1-inch cubes. Combine the squash and the cottage cheese mixture.

4. Spray a baking pan with nonstick vegetable spray and place the squash and cottage cheese mixture in the pan. Sprinkle the bulgur wheat over the casserole evenly. Bake at 400°F for 15 minutes. Serve hot and enjoy.

For 2 servings each serving contains	Calories	324	Fat	3g
	Protein	22g	Cholesterol	5mg
	Carbohydrates	61g	Sodium	673mg

For 3 servings each serving contains	Calories	216	Fat	2g
	Protein	14g	Cholesterol	3mg
	Carbohydrates	41g	Sodium	448mg

It's Not Spaghetti Casserole ➤

We've had a lot of fun watching people's faces as they eat this dish. It really looks like noodles, but it's not. Since it's not, it's much lighter and less filling than pasta. Add some hearty bread for a great pregame meal.

1/2 of an 8-inch spaghetti squash
Nonstick cooking spray
1 medium onion, chopped
6 large fresh mushrooms, sliced (1 1/2 cups)
1 large clove garlic, crushed
1/8 teaspoon pepper
1/4 teaspoon dried oregano
2 tablespoons chopped fresh parsley
1/2 teaspoon dried basil
Dash thyme
1 fresh tomato, chopped
1/2 cup fine bread crumbs
4 ounces 2%-fat cottage cheese
1/2 cup shredded nonfat mozzarella (part-skim-milk mozzarella is lower in sodium but higher in fat)
2 tablespoons grated Parmesan

1. Preheat oven to 375°F. Slice the squash in half lengthwise, scoop out the seeds, and place cut side down in microwave-safe dish. Fill dish with 1/4 inch of water and cover with microwave-safe plastic wrap, leaving one corner unsealed. Cook on high for 15 minutes, or until squash is tender and easily pierced by a fork. Let cool. (Although we prefer the microwave method, you can also cook the squash conventionally. Place the squash cut side down in an oven-safe dish with 1/2 inch of water. Cover and cook in a 375°F oven for 35 to 40 minutes.)

2. While the squash cooks, spray a nonstick frying pan with cooking spray and heat on medium-high heat for 30 seconds. Sauté the onion, mushrooms, garlic, pepper, and herbs over medium heat until the onion is translucent. Turn the heat down to medium-low, add the tomato, and cook until most of the liquid is gone, 5 to 8 minutes.

3. Scoop out the cooked squash into a bowl. Add the sautéed mixture, bread crumbs, cottage cheese, and mozzarella and mix well.

4. Lightly coat a small casserole with a spray of cooking oil. Turn mixture into the casserole and top with Parmesan. Bake at 375°F for 15 to 20 minutes.

For 2 servings	Calories	297	Fat	5g
each serving contains	Protein	25g	Cholesterol	15mg
	Carbohydrates	41g	Sodium	748mg

For 3 servings	Calories	198	Fat	3g
each serving contains	Protein	17g	Cholesterol	10mg
	Carbohydrates	27g	Sodium	498mg

Pacific Rim Kale ➤

Greens are a fabulous source of nutrients, especially the important antioxidant beta-carotene. If you've never had kale or Swiss chard, this is a great way to try them. Serve as a side dish to the Grilled Steak Sandwich (page 156).

6 large leaves of kale (Swiss chard may be subsituted)
1/2 cup water
1 teaspoon soy sauce (low-sodium if desired)
1 tablespoon seasoned rice vinegar

1. Wash the kale thoroughly and trim the leafy portion from the stem. Discard the stem. Bring the water to a boil in a medium saucepan. Add the kale, soy sauce, and rice vinegar. Cover and steam for 10 to 15 minutes, or until kale is tender.

For 2 servings	Calories	103	Fat	1g
each serving contains	Protein	7g	Cholesterol	0mg
	Carbohydrates	21g	Sodium	258mg

For 3 servings	Calories	67	Fat	<1g
each serving contains	Protein	5g	Cholesterol	0mg
	Carbohydrates	14g	Sodium	172mg

Lentil Pâté on Pumpernickel Rye ➤

This is a great sandwich to stick into your backpack before hitting the trail. Lentils are high on the list of healthful foods and this is a tasty way to add them to your diet.

¹/₄ cup dried lentils
³/₄ cup water
1 hard-boiled egg, yolk discarded
¹/₂ large onion
¹/₂ tablespoon canola oil
¹/₄ cup chopped walnuts
Salt and freshly ground black pepper to taste
4 slices pumpernickel rye bread (6 slices for 3 servings)

1. Boil the lentils in water in a covered pan for 30 minutes, until the lentils are soft and all the water has been absorbed.

2. Slice the onion and sauté in the canola oil over medium heat for 5 to 8 minutes, until soft.

3. Blend the lentils, egg, onion, walnuts, salt, and pepper in a blender or food processor until smooth, possibly several minutes. Serve on rye bread, open-faced or closed, at room temperature. This recipe also makes a great appetizer when served with snack-size bread. It is best if made one day ahead and stored, covered, in the refrigerator overnight.

For 2 servings each serving contains	Calories	396	Fat	13g
	Protein	19g	Cholesterol	<1mg
	Carbohydrates	55g	Sodium	537mg

For 3 servings each serving contains	Calories	316	Fat	9g
	Protein	14g	Cholesterol	<1mg
	Carbohydrates	48g	Sodium	479mg

Baked Asparagus ➤

The body builders that I counsel love this recipe because asparagus naturally helps rid the body of excess fluids. Asparagus is also a great source of chromium, important for helping maintain normal blood-sugar levels. And the dish tastes great, too. (SMK)

2/3 pound fresh asparagus spears
1 1/2 cloves garlic, minced
Olive oil cooking spray

1. Preheat oven to 375°F. Wash asparagus and trim the stems.

2. In a small, oven-safe baking pan, place one layer of asparagus. Coat lightly with cooking spray and sprinkle on ⅓ of the garlic. Add another layer of asparagus and repeat until all the asparagus is used.

3. Place in the oven for 10 minutes. Watch closely. The asparagus should be firm and not limp when done.

For 2 servings
each serving contains

Calories	42	Fat	1g
Protein	5g	Cholesterol	0mg
Carbohydrates	6g	Sodium	3mg

For 3 servings
each serving contains

Calories	28	Fat	<1g
Protein	3g	Cholesterol	0mg
Carbohydrates	4g	Sodium	2mg

Marinated Grilled Eggplant ➤

Yes! Eggplant can be served naked without tomato sauce and cheese. This low-calorie dish can be virtually fat free if you drop the small amount of oil in the recipe. It makes a great side dish or a nice filling for a vegetarian sandwich at a barbecue.

1 medium eggplant
¹/₄ cup balsamic vinegar
1 clove garlic, minced
2 teaspoons dry sherry
¹/₂ teaspoon olive oil

1. Slice the eggplant into ½-inch-thick steaks.

2. Combine the vinegar, garlic, sherry, and oil and mix until blended. Place the eggplant steaks in the marinade and coat the eggplant. You can let the eggplant marinate for up to half an hour, but no less than 5 minutes.

3. Cook on an outdoor grill (or place under the broiler) until lightly browned, about 4 minutes. Turn eggplant over and brown the other side. Serve hot with balsamic vinegar as a sauce.

For 2 servings each serving contains				
Calories	38	Fat	1g
Protein	<1g	Cholesterol	0mg
Carbohydrates	6g	Sodium	3mg

For 3 servings each serving contains				
Calories	25	Fat	<1g
Protein	<1g	Cholesterol	0mg
Carbohydrates	4g	Sodium	2mg

Grilled Tomato ➤

This side dish is an excellent source of vitamin C, an important antioxidant. It is a perfect accompaniment to any of the beef dishes in this book.

1 large tomato
¹/₄ cup bulgur wheat
4 sprigs fresh parsley, chopped
¹/₈ cup Yogurt Cheese (page 53)
2 tablespoons grated Parmesan cheese

1. Cut the tomato into ¼-inch slices and arrange them on a cookie sheet. Combine the bulgur wheat, parsley, and cheeses together. Crumble the mixture on top of the tomato slices.

2. Broil the tomato until the topping begins to brown.

Serve hot.

For 2 servings
each serving contains

Calories	96	Fat	2g
Protein	6g	Cholesterol	4mg
Carbohydrates	15g	Sodium	112mg

For 3 servings
each serving contains

Calories	64	Fat	1g
Protein	4g	Cholesterol	3mg
Carbohydrates	10g	Sodium	75mg

Ratatouille ➤

This classic Mediterranean vegetable recipe has been adapted to reduce both fat and cooking time. It is an excellent electrolyte-replacer, since it is high in potassium. This dish is also high in vitamins A and C as well as folic acid.

¹/₂ teaspoon olive oil
1 teaspoon basil
1 teaspoon oregano
1 clove garlic, minced
1 bay leaf
1 small onion, minced
1 small zucchini, cubed
1 yellow summer squash, cubed

1 tomato, cubed

¹/₄ cup tomato juice

Salt and freshly ground pepper to taste

1. Heat the oil with the the basil, oregano, garlic, and bay leaf in a frying pan over medium heat. Add the onion and sauté for 5 minutes. Add the zucchini, yellow squash, tomatoes, and tomato juice. Stir, cover, and simmer for 5 minutes. Uncover and continue to simmer until the vegetables are tender, about 15 minutes.

2. Remove the bay leaf and add salt and freshly ground black pepper to taste.

For 2 servings each serving contains	Calories	73	Fat	2g
	Protein	3g	Cholesterol	0mg
	Carbohydrates	14g	Sodium	121mg

For 3 servings each serving contains	Calories	49	Fat	1g
	Protein	2g	Cholesterol	0mg
	Carbohydrates	9g	Sodium	81mg

Sweet Wheat Pizza ➤

Classic American pizza bears little resemblance to the Italian version, and our low-fat recipe is different from both. Sweeter and chewier, this pizza is a unique treat. To further reduce the fat content, simply replace the mozzarella with fat-free mozzarella. This reduces the fat content by 36 grams for the whole recipe.

1 cup warm water

¹/₄ cup brown sugar

1 envelope dry yeast

1¹/₂ cups whole-wheat flour

1¹/₂ cups all-purpose flour

2 tablespoons olive oil

14-ounce can diced tomatoes, drained

1 tablespoon oregano

1 teaspoon garlic powder

1 teaspoon basil

8-ounce package shredded mozzarella

4 ounces mushrooms, sliced

¹/₂ small onion, chopped

¹/₄ green pepper, chopped

1. Combine the water, sugar, and yeast, cover with plastic wrap, and let stand for 5 minutes.

2. Combine the whole-wheat flour and all-purpose flour in a large bowl. Make a small well in the center and pour the yeast mixture into it. Add 1 tablespoon of the oil, reserving the rest to oil the pan. Slowly add flour from the sides of the bowl into the yeast mixture. Continue until all of the flour has been incorporated into the dough.

3. Knead the dough on a floured surface until it becomes elastic, about 5 minutes. Form into a ball. Return the dough to the bowl and cover. Let dough rise in a warm place until you are ready to use it (it's best if you can let the dough rise for ½ to 1 hour). Oil a 9-inch cake pan and set it aside for later use.

4. Flatten the ball of dough with your hand. Press the dough into the pan, starting in the middle and then pressing outward with your fingers until the bottom of the pan is completely covered. Sprinkle the tomatoes, oregano, garlic, and basil on top of the dough. Cover with the cheese. Complete by adding the mushrooms, onion, and green pepper.

5. Bake in a 450°F oven for 15 minutes until golden brown.

For 2 servings each serving contains	Calories	1,237	Fat	35g
	Protein	58g	Cholesterol	65mg
	Carbohydrates	182g	Sodium	570mg

For 3 servings each serving contains	Calories	825	Fat	23g
	Protein	39g	Cholesterol	43mg
	Carbohydrates	122g	Sodium	380mg

Vegetable Yamcakes ➤

This is a fragrant, wonderful side dish that is high in antioxidants as well as an excellent source of potassium for electrolyte replacement.

1 large yam, grated

¹/₄ cup frozen corn kernels, defrosted

1 scallion, minced

²/₃ carrot, chopped

¹/₈ cup chopped sun-dried tomatoes (3 whole), rehydrated in ¼ cup hot water

¹/₈ cup bulgur wheat or fat-free bread crumbs

¹/₂ teaspoon garlic powder

2 egg whites

1 whole egg

Nonstick vegetable spray

1. Combine the grated yam, corn kernels, scallion, and carrot. Drain the tomatoes and add them to the other vegetables. Add the bulgur wheat and garlic powder.

2. Beat the egg whites and whole egg together with a fork until slightly frothy. Add the egg to the vegetables and mix until all vegetables are coated.

3. Spray a nonstick pan with vegetable spray and heat it on high for 1 minute. Reduce the heat to medium. Drop spoonfuls of batter onto the pan and flatten slightly. Cook the patties on one side until browned, 5 to 7 minutes. Turn the patties over with a spatula and cook on the other side until browned, an additional 5 minutes. Serve hot, or use as a cold snack when out hiking or biking. They will keep for several hours at room temperature and for a few days in the refrigerator, or you can freeze them for up to a month.

For 2 servings each serving contains				
Calories	395	Fat	3g
Protein	13g	Cholesterol	106mg
Carbohydrates	80g	Sodium	122mg

For 3 servings each serving contains				
Calories	263	Fat	2g
Protein	9g	Cholesterol	71mg
Carbohydrates	53g	Sodium	81mg

6

Success at **SEA** Seafood

Pan-fried Cajun Catfish ➤

I was so excited when I realized that one could have crisp fried fish without all the fat that I made this dish at 10 o'clock at night, just to see if it would work. I think you'll love it. (SMK)

$^1/_2$ cup cornmeal
1 teaspoon dried parsley flakes
$^1/_2$ teaspoon paprika
$^1/_8$ teaspoon cayenne pepper
$^1/_8$ teaspoon white pepper
$^1/_8$ teaspoon black pepper
$^1/_2$ teaspoon salt
$^1/_4$ teaspoon thyme
$^1/_2$ teaspoon garlic powder
$^1/_4$ teaspoon onion powder
1 egg
2 $^1/_2$ tablespoons water
12 ounces farm-raised catfish fillets
Nonstick cooking spray
$^1/_2$ fresh lemon, cut into wedges

1. Mix together the cornmeal, herbs, and spices in a flat dish. In a separate dish beat the egg with the water.

2. Clean the fish.

3. Heat a nonstick frying pan over medium-high heat for 30 seconds. Generously spray the pan with cooking spray. Dip each fillet in the egg-water mixture and then coat generously in the cornmeal mixture. Place in the frying pan, skin side down, for 5 to 6 minutes, or until the bottom is golden brown. Turn the fish and cook another 6 to 7 minutes. Turn again if needed and remove promptly. Watch the fish closely as it cooks. Do not let the oil smoke or the coating burn. Fish should be tender inside, crisp and brown on the outside. Serve hot with lemon wedges.

For 2 servings each serving contains	Calories	320	Fat	9g
	Protein	34g	Cholesterol	109mg
	Carbohydrates	24g	Sodium	378mg

For 3 servings each serving contains	Calories	214	Fat	6g
	Protein	23g	Cholesterol	73mg
	Carbohydrates	16g	Sodium	252mg

Baked Flounder with Vegetables ➤

Fish oils are necessary in our diet to maintain heart health. You should eat a minimum of two fish meals per week. This dish is delicious and pretty to serve to guests.

1 medium onion
1 green pepper
1 slicing tomato
12 ounces flounder fillets
2 tablespoons fresh lemon juice
4 mushrooms, sliced
1/2 teaspoon black pepper
1 1/2 teaspoons garlic powder
1/2 teaspoon salt
1/4 cup freshly grated Parmesan cheese

1. Preheat oven to 425°F. Slice the onion, green pepper, and tomato into rings.

2. Clean the fish. Place the fillets on a baking sheet and sprinkle with lemon juice. Place the onion, green pepper, tomato, and mushrooms on top of and around the fillets, in the order listed. Sprinkle black pepper, garlic, salt, and Parmesan cheese all over the top of the preparation.

3. Cover and bake for 15 to 20 minutes. Uncover for the last 2 minutes and turn on the broiler to brown the Parmesan. Remove promptly. Do not let the Parmesan burn.

For 2 servings
each serving contains

Calories	266	Fat	6g
Protein	39g	Cholesterol	89mg
Carbohydrates	16g	Sodium	867mg

For 3 servings
each serving contains

Calories	178	Fat	4g
Protein	26g	Cholesterol	60mg
Carbohydrates	10g	Sodium	578mg

Oriental Halibut ➤

Scientists believe that oils found in cold-water fish like halibut, salmon, and mackerel have kept Eskimos safe from heart disease despite their high-fat diet. Halibut is a tasty fish, and this recipe can be enjoyed by fish lovers and non-fish-lovers alike. A wonderful accompaniment to this dish is Champion Noodles (page 63).

2 ounces apple cider or apple juice
2 tablespoons soy sauce
¹/₂ tablespoon sesame oil
1 clove garlic, minced
¹/₂ teaspoon minced fresh ginger
12 ounces halibut steaks or fillets

1. Mix together the cider, soy sauce, oil, garlic, and ginger.

2. Clean the halibut. Place in a small pan and cover with the soy sauce mixture. Marinate for 20 to 30 minutes.

3. Broil the halibut for 8 to 10 minutes, depending on thickness of the fish. Watch carefully. Do not let the marinade burn. The steaks do not need to be turned during cooking.

For 2 servings
each serving contains

Calories	202	Fat	5g
Protein	36g	Cholesterol	54mg
Carbohydrates	1g	Sodium	349mg

For 3 servings
each serving contains

Calories	135	Fat	3g
Protein	24g	Cholesterol	36mg
Carbohydrates	<1g	Sodium	233mg

Simple Salmon ➤

This dish is so good and so easy that you won't believe it. And salmon is a great source of the healthful fish oils that we need. Add some steamed vegetables and rice to complete the meal.

³/₄ pound salmon fillets

2 tablespoons lemon juice

¹/₄ teaspoon dried dillweed

1. Place the salmon in a microwave-safe dish. Sprinkle with lemon juice and then dill. Cover dish with plastic wrap, leaving an open vent.

2. Cook in microwave on medium power for 4 minutes, or until fish is cooked through and flaky but not dry. (Microwave ovens vary in power, so cooking times may vary.) Allow fish to sit in dish for 30 to 60 seconds after cooking. (You can also broil the fish for 10 to 12 minutes on a broiler pan. If you do, however, a small amount of oil needs to be added for moistness.)

For 2 servings
each serving contains

Calories	207	Fat	6g
Protein	34g	Cholesterol	126mg
Carbohydrates	1g	Sodium	85mg

For 3 servings
each serving contains

Calories	138	Fat	4g
Protein	23g	Cholesterol	84mg
Carbohydrates	<1g	Sodium	57mg

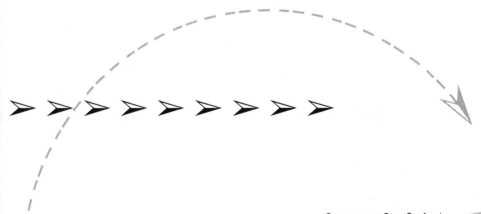

Mint Mango Salmon ➤

Northwestern salmon meets the tropics. This unique medley of flavors is sweet yet has a bite. The mango is an excellent source of antioxidants, which may help prevent cancer and lessen the effects of aging.

1 pound salmon steaks

Fresh lemon juice

1 very ripe fresh mango, cubed, or 1-quart jar mango slices, drained and cubed

¹/₂ cup water

1 small, mild chili pepper, seeded and finely sliced

2 tablespoons minced fresh mint

1. Drizzle the lemon juice over the salmon steaks. Broil the salmon approximately 7 minutes on each side.

2. Meanwhile, combine the mango, water, and chili pepper and cook in a saucepan over high heat until the mango is soft or the water has been absorbed. Add the mint to the sauce and allow to simmer for about 5 minutes.

3. When the salmon is cooked, place on a platter, pour the sauce over the salmon, and garnish with fresh mint. Or place the sauce on the platter first and put the salmon on top.

For 2 servings
each serving contains

Calories	345	Fat	8g
Protein	47g	Cholesterol	121mg
Carbohydrates	20g	Sodium	159mg

For 3 servings
each serving contains

Calories	230	Fat	6g
Protein	31g	Cholesterol	80mg
Carbohydrates	13g	Sodium	106mg

Lemon Strawberry Snapper ➤

This recipe is incredible. If Monet were still alive, he would paint it. This impressionistic food version of sunset is an excellent source of calcium, manganese, and electrolytes. It is a wonderful way to replenish yourself both physically and mentally after a big race or a hard day at the office.

3 tablespoons cornstarch dissolved in ¹/₂ cup cold water
1 cup water
¹/₂ cup sugar
Juice of **2** lemons
1 egg yolk, beaten
²/₃ pound red snapper fillets
Paprika
¹/₂ pound angel hair pasta
3 scallions, minced
4 large strawberries, sliced

1. Combine the cornstarch mixture, water, sugar, and lemon juice. Cook over high heat, mixing to prevent scorching, until thickened, about 5 minutes. Add the egg yolk and allow to simmer an additional 2 minutes.

2. Meanwhile, place the fish, skin side down, into an ungreased nonstick baking dish and sprinkle with paprika. Bake at 400°F for 15 minutes, or until white and flaky.

3. Cook the angel hair pasta according to package directions and drain. Place the drained pasta on a platter.

4. Add the scallions and strawberries to the lemon sauce and mix thoroughly. Simmer for 1 minute. Place the cooked fish on top of the pasta and spoon the lemon sauce over it. Serve immediately.

For 2 servings
each serving contains

Calories	837	Fat	8g
Protein	51g	Cholesterol	253mg
Carbohydrates	141g	Sodium	152mg

For 3 servings
each serving contains

Calories	558	Fat	5g
Protein	34g	Cholesterol	169mg
Carbohydrates	94g	Sodium	102mg

Lemon Sole with Mustard Sauce ➤

This "sole-ful" low-calorie treat is a perfect light meal for warm evenings. To increase the carbohydrate content, serve with Caramelized Jerusalem Artichokes (page 70). This dish, high in vitamin B-6, vitamin B-12, and niacin, is a wonderful B-vitamin booster.

1 pound lemon sole fillets
¹/₄ cup lemon juice
¹/₄ cup white wine

Mustard Sauce

1 teaspoon cornstarch dissolved in ¹/₈ cup cold water
1 cup water
¹/₄ cup apple juice
2 teaspoons dry white wine
1 teaspoon garlic
1 tablespoon lime juice sweetened with 1 teaspoon sugar
2 teaspoons prepared yellow mustard
1 teaspoon Worcestershire sauce
¹/₈ teaspoon cayenne pepper

1. Place the fish, lemon juice, and ¹/₄ cup white wine in a pan and bake at 400°F for 20 minutes, or until the fish is flaky and white.

2. Combine the dissolved cornstarch, water, apple juice, 2 teaspoons wine, and garlic in a saucepan. Heat over medium heat to thicken, stirring often.

3. Combine the sweetened lime juice, mustard, Worcestershire sauce, and cayenne pepper. Add the mustard mixture to the cornstarch mixture and stir until well blended. Allow the mixture to continue cooking until thickened.

4. Place the fish on a platter, pour the mustard sauce over it and serve.

For 2 servings each serving contains	Calories	345	Fat	8g
	Protein	48g	Cholesterol	132mg
	Carbohydrates	12g	Sodium	125mg

For 3 servings each serving contains	Calories	230	Fat	5g
	Protein	32g	Cholesterol	88mg
	Carbohydrates	8g	Sodium	84mg

Artichoke-Stuffed Trout ➤

This pumped-up trout is easy to make and looks wonderful. It goes well with
Rice and Vermicelli (page 72) to balance your carbohydrate load. This dish is
high in B vitamins like niacin, B-2, B-6, and B-12.

Nonstick vegetable spray
14-ounce can artichoke hearts in brine, drained and sliced
8 to **10** shallots, peeled and minced
2 ounces mushrooms, sliced
1/4 cup white wine
1/4 teaspoon freshly ground black pepper
1 pound rainbow trout fillets

1. Spray a nonstick pan with nonstick vegetable spray. Combine the artichokes,
   shallots, and mushrooms in the pan and cook them with the wine and pepper,
   stirring occasionally, for 10 minutes over medium heat.

2. Place the trout in a baking pan sprayed with nonstick vegetable spray. Spoon
   some of the artichoke filling into the center of each fillet, and fold the fillet to
   cover the filling.

3. Place the trout in a 400°F oven and bake for ½ hour, or until the fish is firm
   and flaky. Serve immediately.

For 2 servings
each serving contains

Calories	361	Fat	9g
Protein	53g	Cholesterol	132mg
Carbohydrates	19g	Sodium	124mg

For 3 servings
each serving contains

Calories	241	Fat	6g
Protein	35g	Cholesterol	88mg
Carbohydrates	12g	Sodium	82mg

Oven-Fried Perch

For a classic fish-and-chips meal, try matching this dish with First Place Fries (page 67). The tangy cocktail sauce recipe makes a wonderful dip—the major culinary gift from the British Isles. This is an excellent source of potassium, magnesium, and calcium, important electrolytes for maintaining fluid balance and nerve conduction.

1/2 cup whole-wheat flour
2 teaspoons paprika
1/2 teaspoon garlic powder
1/4 teaspoon dried parsley flakes
1/8 teaspoon pepper
3/4 pound ocean perch fillets
Nonstick vegetable spray
1 recipe Cocktail Sauce (recipe follows)

1. Combine the flour, paprika, garlic powder, parsley flakes, and pepper in a plastic bag. Shake the bag to mix the ingredients.

2. Rinse the fish in cold water and put a few pieces into the plastic bag. Shake the bag until the fish is coated. Place the fish on a baking dish. Continue until all the pieces have been coated. Spray the fish lightly with nonstick vegetable spray.

3. Bake the fish at 400°F for 20 minutes, or until the fish is golden brown. Serve with Cocktail Sauce.

For 2 servings
each serving contains

Calories	331	Fat	2.4g
Protein	39g	Cholesterol	156mg
Carbohydrates	39g	Sodium	802mg

For 3 servings
each serving contains

Calories	221	Fat	1.6g
Protein	26g	Cholesterol	104mg
Carbohydrates	27g	Sodium	535mg

The **High Performance** Cookbook

Cocktail Sauce

1 stalk celery, minced
1 teaspoon white horseradish
¹/₂ cup catsup

1. Combine the celery, horseradish, and catsup. Chill until needed. This can remain in the refrigerator for up to a week.

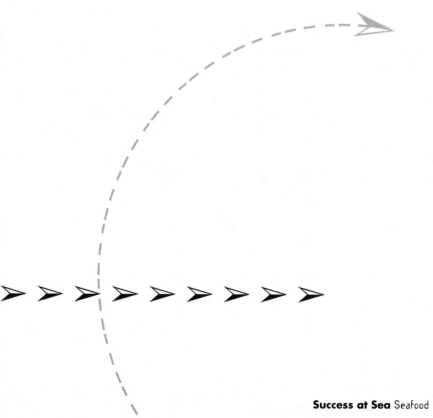

Scallops with Ginger Scallion Sauce ➤

This pungent dish can be made not only with scallops but with any fish or poultry. It is a classic Oriental dish when served with rice, or you can use noodles instead. It is an excellent electrolyte replenisher.

1 tablespoon oil

1 teaspoon minced garlic

3 scallions, minced

5 slices fresh ginger about the size of a quarter and $^1/_8$-inch thick, peeled and minced

3/4 pound scallops, rinsed and patted dry

4 ounces mushrooms, sliced

1 tablespoon cornstarch dissolved in $^1/_4$ cup cold water

1 teaspoon sugar

2 tablespoons soy sauce

2 cups cooked rice

1. Cook the garlic, scallions, and ginger in the oil over medium heat, stirring, for about 2 minutes. Add the scallops and mushrooms and continue to cook for 5 more minutes.

2. Combine the cornstarch mixture, sugar, and soy sauce and pour over the scallops. Cook for an additional 3 minutes, or until the sauce becomes shiny. Serve immediately over rice.

For 2 servings
each serving contains

Calories	505	Fat	11g
Protein	37g	Cholesterol	57mg
Carbohydrates	65g	Sodium	1,327mg

For 3 servings
each serving contains

Calories	337	Fat	7g
Protein	24g	Cholesterol	38mg
Carbohydrates	42g	Sodium	885mg

Seafood Stir-Fry ➤

This is a great one-pot dinner. Serve tea with the meal, and a light dessert of fresh fruit and sorbet. Put leftovers in a microwave-safe container for reheating at work the next day.

8 ounces frozen medium shrimp

1/2 cup parboiled brown rice (Minute Rice, Uncle Ben's, etc.) or long-cooking brown rice if you have the time

1 cup water

1 pound precut fresh stir-fry vegetables (broccoli, pea pods, mushrooms, bean sprouts, etc.)

1 1/2 tablespoons canola oil

3 cloves garlic, minced

1 teaspoon freshly grated ginger

1 tablespoon soy sauce

1 tablespoon cornstarch dissolved in 2 tablespoons cold water

1. Defrost the shrimp according to package directions. Begin to cook the rice in water according to package directions. Rinse and drain the vegetables.

2. Put ¹/₂ tablespoon of the oil into a nonstick wok or frying pan and heat over medium. When the oil is hot, add half of the garlic and cook about 40 seconds. Increase the heat to medium-high and add the shrimp. Stir continuously and cook just until the shrimp are pink and curled, about 4 minutes. Remove the shrimp.

3. Put remaining tablespoon of oil into the wok and heat over medium heat. Add remaining garlic and cook for 40 seconds. Increase the heat to high, add the vegetables, and stir continuously for 4 minutes.

4. Add the ginger and stir for 2 more minutes. Add the soy sauce and mix well. Add the cornstarch mixture and continue stirring for 2 minutes, until the vegetables are cooked but still crisp and brightly colored and the sauce is slightly thickened. Toss in the shrimp and serve over rice.

For 2 servings each serving contains				
	Calories	502	Fat	14g
	Protein	31g	Cholesterol	172mg
	Carbohydrates	62g	Sodium	700mg

For 3 servings each serving contains				
	Calories	333	Fat	9g
	Protein	21g	Cholesterol	115mg
	Carbohydrates	41g	Sodium	467mg

Swordfish Kabobs ➢

This dish has been a big hit with people who like to grill at the beach. It just has that summery taste to it. If you take it to the beach, make sure to keep the fish on ice until you cook it.

1/2 cup parboiled brown rice (Minute Rice, Uncle Ben's, etc.) or long-cooking brown rice if you have the time

Marinade

1/4 cup water
1/4 cup seasoned rice vinegar
1/2 teaspoon soy sauce
1 teaspoon sesame oil
1 tablespoon lemon juice
1/2 teaspoon minced ginger
1/2 teaspoon dried tarragon
1/4 teaspoon dried rosemary
1/2 teaspoon garlic powder
Pinch freshly ground black pepper

To complete the dish

1/2 green pepper
1/2 red pepper
1 onion
1/2 pound swordfish, cubed
24 green seedless grapes
Eight 6- or 10-inch skewers

1. Preheat a grill. Cook the rice according to package directions.

2. Mix together all the marinade ingredients. Set aside.

3. Cut peppers and onion into large chunks. Place all the ingredients on skewers, beginning and ending each skewer with a piece of pepper and alternating all other ingredients. The grapes work well on either side of the fish. Two pieces of fish should fit on each skewer.

4. Place the skewers in a dish and cover with the marinade for 15 minutes, basting several times. (You can prepare the recipe up to this point in the morning, and let the kabobs marinate in the refrigerator all day.)

5. Grill over medium-high heat. Periodically drizzle with leftover marinade, and turn after 5 minutes. Cook for 10 minutes on gas grill, or until done over charcoal. Kabobs may also be cooked under the broiler following the same directions. Serve over rice.

For 2 servings
each serving contains

Calories	361	Fat	7g
Protein	27g	Cholesterol	44mg
Carbohydrates	48g	Sodium	125mg

For 3 servings
each serving contains

Calories	240	Fat	4g
Protein	18g	Cholesterol	30mg
Carbohydrates	32g	Sodium	83mg

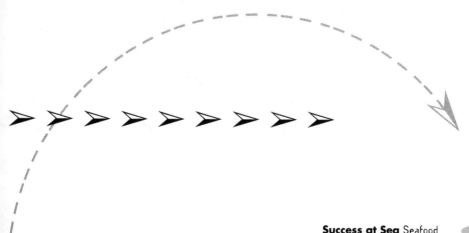

Key West Fish Salad ➤

This dish is perfect when you need protein but don't want to feel weighed down. This recipe actually works well with any fish. You can also use leftover fish with these ingredients as a great way to recycle last night's dinner. It is as delectable as a restaurant salad, but with half the fat. I have also used this as an hors d'oeuvre with rave reviews. (KRFK)

³/₄ pound white fish fillets

¹/₃ cup lime juice

2 stalks celery, chopped

1 onion, minced

2 carrots, chopped

1 teaspoon dillweed

¹/₂ teaspoon tarragon

¹/₄ cup low-fat mayonnaise

2 whole-wheat rolls (3 for 3 servings)

1. Bake the fish in a single layer covered with lime juice at 400°F for 15 minutes, or until flaky and white.

2. Combine the celery, onion, carrots, dillweed, tarragon, and mayonnaise.

3. When the fish is done, cut it into cubes and allow to cool slightly. Combine the fish with the vegetable mixture and chill until you are ready to serve. Serve on the rolls.

For 2 servings
each serving contains

Calories	602	Fat	10g
Protein	57g	Cholesterol	212mg
Carbohydrates	74g	Sodium	1,043mg

For 3 servings
each serving contains

Calories	487	Fat	8g
Protein	41g	Cholesterol	142mg
Carbohydrates	67g	Sodium	883mg

The **High Performance** Cookbook

Vegetable Tuna ➤

This easy and quick tuna treat is a flavorful change from traditional tuna salad. The vegetables add both color and texture, as well as beta-carotene, an important antioxidant.

6- to **7-**ounce can tuna packed in water, drained
1 stalk celery, minced
3 radishes, minced
1 large carrot, minced
2 scallions, minced
¹/₄ cup low-fat mayonnaise
2 tablespoons (1 ounce) Yogurt Cheese (page 53)
Juice of **¹/₂** lemon
2 whole-wheat rolls (3 for 3 servings)

1. Mash the tuna with a fork. Add the minced celery, radishes, carrot, and scallions. Mix until well blended.

2. Blend the mayonnaise with the yogurt cheese. Add the lemon juice, combine well, pour the dressing on the tuna, and mix until tuna is well coated.

3. Chill for a minimum of 10 minutes but preferably longer, up to 45 minutes. Serve on a whole wheat roll.

For 2 servings
each serving contains

Calories	416	Fat	10g
Protein	32g	Cholesterol	39mg
Carbohydrates	53g	Sodium	1,071mg

For 3 servings
each serving contains

Calories	341	Fat	7g
Protein	25g	Cholesterol	48mg
Carbohydrates	48g	Sodium	860mg

Popeye's Delight ➤

This great high-carbohydrate dish is packed with protein and the antioxidant beta-carotene. It is teeming with iron, potassium, folic acid, and magnesium and is a good source of calcium and phosphorus. Preparation is quick and easy, and it's a meal in itself. We suggest using frozen spinach so that you can have all the ingredients on hand; additionally, fresh spinach is often difficult to wash thoroughly. If you do use fresh spinach, chop it finely. You may have to slightly increase the cooking time to evaporate the liquid in step 4.

10-ounce box frozen chopped spinach (or about 1 pound fresh; see note above)

1 cup boiling water

20 sun-dried tomato halves (1 ounce), chopped

2 tablespoons olive oil

3 cloves garlic, chopped

12 ounces medium shrimp, peeled and deveined

1/8 teaspoon freshly ground black pepper

1/2 pound dried tomato fettucini

2 tablespoons grated Parmesan cheese (3 tablespoons for 3 servings)

Freshly ground black pepper

1. Defrost the spinach by removing it from the box and placing it in a colander. Rinse briefly with cool water. Using a fork, break it into pieces so that it will defrost more quickly. Set aside.

2. Soak the sun-dried tomatoes in boiling water for 5 minutes to soften. In a nonstick pan heat the oil over medium-high heat for 45 seconds. Add the garlic and cook for 30 seconds, then add the shrimp. Season with black pepper and cook for 3 minutes, stirring frequently. Remove the shrimp from the pan with a slotted spoon and set aside.

3. Cook the pasta in boiling water for 8 minutes or according to package directions and drain.

4. Meanwhile, return the nonstick pan to medium-high heat. Drain the defrosted spinach and add to the pan. Add the chopped dried tomatoes and sauté, stirring continuously, for 1 minute, or until the liquid has evaporated and the mixture is hot but not limp. Add the shrimp and stir for 30 seconds.

5. Spoon the shrimp and spinach over the pasta. Season with black pepper and sprinkle each serving with 1 tablespoon Parmesan cheese.

For 2 servings each serving contains	Calories	787	Fat	20g
	Protein	56g	Cholesterol	262mg
	Carbohydrates	94g	Sodium	459mg

For 3 servings each serving contains	Calories	532	Fat	14g
	Protein	38g	Cholesterol	176mg
	Carbohydrates	63g	Sodium	337mg

Shrimp Roll ➤

The shrimp roll is a classic dish up and down the American East Coast. This version simply gets rid of some of the fat. Remember that shrimp is an excellent source of omega-3 fatty acids. Take a bite and hear the surf!

¹/₂ pound cooked and shelled popcorn shrimp, or larger shrimp chopped into ¹/₂-inch pieces

2 stalks celery, diced

1 hard-boiled egg, diced

¹/₄ cup low-fat mayonnaise

¹/₈ teaspoon cayenne pepper

¹/₄ teaspoon tarragon

Juice of **¹/₂** lemon

2 soft rolls (3 for 3 servings)

1. Combine the shrimp, celery, and egg. Add the mayonnaise, cayenne, tarragon, and lemon juice and mix thoroughly. Chill the salad for at least 10 minutes but preferably longer, up to 45 minutes. Load into the rolls and enjoy!

For 2 servings each serving contains	Calories	561	Fat	17g
	Protein	38g	Cholesterol	335mg
	Carbohydrates	67g	Sodium	1,434mg

For 3 servings each serving contains	Calories	460	Fat	12g
	Protein	29g	Cholesterol	224mg
	Carbohydrates	62g	Sodium	1,144mg

Shrimp Creole ➤

Traditional shrimp creole is a favorite of New Orleans. This easy, three-step version gives you the option of using okra, a flavorful dark green vegetable common in southern cooking. Okra is an excellent source of beta-carotene, folic acid, and vitamin K. Although the cholesterol seems high in this recipe, remember that shrimp is an excellent source of omega-3 fatty acids. Laissez les bons temps rouler—*"Let the good times roll!"*

$1/4$ cup canola oil
$1/4$ cup all-purpose flour
$1/2$ small onion, minced
1 stalk celery, minced
2 ounces ($1/2$ cup) chopped fresh or frozen okra (optional)
$1/4$ sweet green bell pepper, minced
2 cloves garlic, minced
$3/4$ cup (6 ounces) canned puréed tomatoes
$1/2$ tomato, diced
1 bay leaf, crumbled
1 clove, ground ($1/8$ teaspoon)
1 cup (8 ounces) fish stock or clam juice
1 pound cooked shrimp, peeled and deveined
1 scallion, chopped
1 ounce (about 20 sprigs) fresh parsley, minced
2 tablespoons (1 ounce) dry white wine
Salt and freshly ground black pepper to taste
2 drops Tabasco (optional)
2 cups cooked brown rice

1. Combine the oil and flour. Mixing continuously with a wire wisk, cook in a saucepan over low heat until the flour is blended and begins to brown, about 15 minutes. Add the onion, celery, okra, green pepper, garlic, puréed tomatoes, diced tomatoes, bay leaf, and clove. Bring to a slow boil, then reduce the heat to low so the mixture simmers.

2. Add the fish stock to the sauce a little at a time, mixing until a smooth, non-runny sauce forms. Add the shrimp, scallion, parsley, wine, salt, pepper, and Tabasco to the sauce and continue to simmer for 5 minutes. Serve over rice.

For 2 servings
each serving contains

Calories	846	Fat	27g
Protein	49g	Cholesterol	339mg
Carbohydrates	100g	Sodium	442mg

For 3 servings
each serving contains

Calories	564	Fat	18g
Protein	32g	Cholesterol	226mg
Carbohydrates	67g	Sodium	294mg

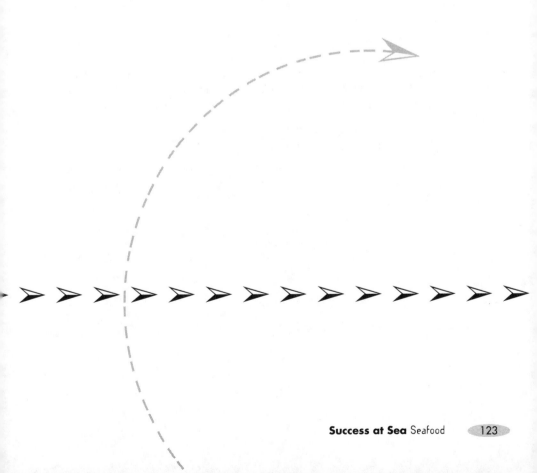

Crab Newburgh ➢

We haven't figured out why this seafood dish is named after a town in the middle of New York state! Kidding aside, they don't have crab on the Hudson River, but this recipe is perfect for entertaining no matter where you are. It is also high in zinc, copper, and magnesium, important minerals in energy metabolism.

1 tablespoon unsalted butter
1 scallion, chopped
1/4 sweet green bell pepper, diced
1 large tomato, peeled and chopped
1/2 pound cooked crabmeat
3 ounces mushrooms, chopped
4 ounces fat-free Swiss cheese
1 tablespoon chopped fresh parsley
1 ounce mozzarella
Dash white pepper
1/2 teaspoon salt
1/4 cup bulgur wheat
Hungarian paprika

1. Melt the butter in a saucepan over medium heat. Add the scallion, green pepper, tomato, and crabmeat and cook, stirring occasionally, for 5 minutes. Add the mushrooms and continue cooking until tender, about 5 minutes more.

2. Add the Swiss cheese, parsley, mozzarella, white pepper, and salt and mix. Slowly add the bulgur wheat while continuing to mix.

3. When the bulgur has been blended, pour into individual oven-safe casserole dishes, sprinkle with paprika, and bake at 400°F for 20 minutes, or until the tops brown.

For 2 servings each serving contains	Calories	364	Fat	11g
	Protein	46g	Cholesterol	90mg
	Carbohydrates	22g	Sodium	1,909mg

For 3 servings each serving contains	Calories	242	Fat	7g
	Protein	31g	Cholesterol	60mg
	Carbohydrates	14g	Sodium	1,273mg

Winged
WINNERS
Poultry

Chicken à l'Orange ➤

This recipe and the next each take an hour total for preparation and cooking, but they take only 15 minutes of your time to prepare before throwing them in the oven to cook on their own. So come home from work, prepare this dish, toss it in the oven, and do an in-home workout for 45 minutes. By the time you're done, dinner will be ready.

1 pound skinless chicken (dark or light meat)
4 medium carrots, cut into chunks
1 small onion, quartered
4 parsnips, cut into chunks
6-ounce can frozen orange juice concentrate
1-ounce envelope Lipton Recipe Secrets dehydrated onion soup mix

1. Preheat oven to 425°F. Clean the chicken and place in an oven-safe casserole. Surround with carrots, onion, and parsnips.

2. Partially defrost the orange juice by holding the unopened can under warm running water. When the concentrate is soft but not watery, open the can and place concentrate in a small mixing bowl. Add the dry soup mix and stir. Pour the mixture over chicken and vegetable casserole. Cover the casserole and place in the oven to cook for 45 minutes.

For 2 servings
each serving contains

Calories	489	Fat	7g
Protein	53g	Cholesterol	160mg
Carbohydrates	54g	Sodium	552mg

For 3 servings
each serving contains

Calories	326	Fat	4g
Protein	35g	Cholesterol	107mg
Carbohydrates	36g	Sodium	368mg

One-Pot Baked Chicken and Vegetable Dinner ➤

This hearty meal is a great wintertime warmer, and it works well on days when you haven't been able to eat enough. It is high in potassium and beta-carotene and will give you almost all the protein you need for a day, plus a good chunk of the carbohydrates.

1 pound skinless chicken (light or dark meat)

4 medium parsnips, cut into chunks

2 small onions, quartered

1 medium yam, cut into chunks

2 medium carrots, cut into chunks

1 teaspoon garlic powder

¹/₈ teaspoon white pepper

¹/₂ teaspoon vegetable-seasoning salt

¹/₂ cup dry vermouth or dry white wine

2 tablespoons chopped fresh parsley

7 ounces fresh refrigerated spinach fettucini

1. Preheat oven to 425°F. Clean the chicken and place in an oven-safe casserole dish. Surround with vegetables.

2. Sprinkle the chicken and vegetables with garlic powder, pepper, seasoning salt, vermouth, and 1 tablespoon of the parsley. Cover and cook in oven for 45 minutes.

3. Cook the fettucini for 2 to 3 minutes in boiling salted water.

4. Remove chicken and vegetables from oven. Serve over fettucini with remaining parsley sprinkled on top.

For 2 servings
each serving contains

Calories	851	Fat	9g
Protein	65g	Cholesterol	230mg
Carbohydrates	125g	Sodium	394mg

For 3 servings
each serving contains

Calories	568	Fat	6g
Protein	43g	Cholesterol	154mg
Carbohydrates	83g	Sodium	262mg

BBQ Chicken ➤

Barbecue recipes are family secrets that are passed down from generation to generation. This one is a low-fat treat that can be shared with everyone. First-Place Fries (page 67) are great with this dish.

1 pound chicken, skinned (light or dark meat)

4 ounces fresh or reconstituted lemon juice

6 tablespoons High-Performance BBQ Sauce (recipe follows)

1. Turn on broiler or grill to medium-high. Clean the chicken and place on broiler pan or grill, sprinkling lightly with lemon juice to keep it from drying out while it cooks.

2. Cook the chicken, periodically turning and sprinkling with lemon juice, until done, about 30 minutes.

3. Brush with High-Performance BBQ Sauce and continue cooking, watching closely so that the sauce bubbles but does not burn. Turn the chicken and brush with the rest of the BBQ sauce. Remove promptly. Total cooking time is approximately 35 to 40 minutes.

For 2 servings
each serving contains

Calories	303	Fat	6g
Protein	50g	Cholesterol	160mg
Carbohydrates	12g	Sodium	505mg

For 3 servings
each serving contains

Calories	202	Fat	4g
Protein	33g	Cholesterol	107mg
Carbohydrates	8g	Sodium	337mg

High-Performance BBQ Sauce

1 cup (8 ounces) tomato purée
2¹/₂ tablespoons orange juice
2 tablespoons honey
1¹/₂ tablespoons soy sauce
1 clove garlic, minced
1 teaspoon brown sugar
¹/₄ teaspoon onion powder
Dash white pepper

1. Mix all the ingredients in a blender for 60 seconds, until well blended. To store leftover sauce, boil the entire recipe for 3 to 5 minutes over high heat. The sauce need not cool before being used. Store in a closed container in the refrigerator for up to two weeks.

   Makes 1¹/₂ cups

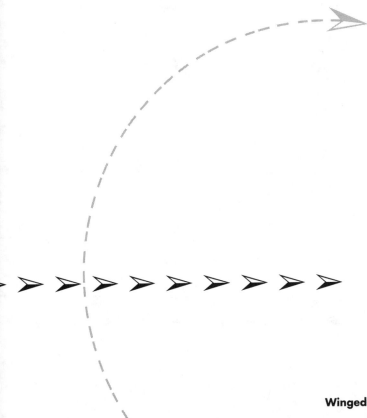

Honey Chicken Dijon ➤

This quick, easy dish is loaded with protein and can be made in the oven or on the grill. The sweet and tangy glaze adds something new to basic grilled chicken. To make it on the grill, simply brush the chicken with the sauce and grill on both sides until done. The Whole-Wheat Pasta Treat on page 58 complements this meal nicely.

³/₄ pound skinless, boneless chicken breast
1 teaspoon paprika
3 tablespoons honey
2 teaspoons Dijon mustard

1. Sprinkle the chicken with the paprika. Place the chicken in a roasting pan and cover. Bake at 400°F for 25 minutes. Drain the excess fat from the chicken.

2. Combine the honey and mustard and brush it on the chicken. Continue cooking the chicken for an additional 10 minutes, or until it begins to brown.

For 2 servings
each serving contains

Calories	289	Fat	2.5g
Protein	40g	Cholesterol	99mg
Carbohydrates	27g	Sodium	172mg

For 3 servings
each serving contains

Calories	193	Fat	1.6g
Protein	26g	Cholesterol	66mg
Carbohydrates	18g	Sodium	114mg

Mint Pineapple Chicken ➤

This extremely low-fat meal is cool, tart, and sweet all in the same bite. It is an excellent source of magnesium and folic acid. So put this in the ring with Sumptuous Stuffing (page 74) for a great one-two punch.

³/₄ pound skinless, boneless chicken breast
Paprika
8-ounce can pineapple chunks in natural juice (reserve juice)
¹/₂ cup additional pineapple juice or citrus juice
1 tablespoon cornstarch dissolved in ¹/₄ cup cold water
¹/₃ cup sugar
1 tablespoon minced fresh mint

1. Place the chicken in a roasting pan, sprinkle with paprika, and cover. Bake at 400°F for 25 minutes.

2. While the chicken is cooking, drain the pineapple, reserving the juice. Combine the reserved pineapple juice and the additional ¹/₂ cup juice in a saucepan. Add the cornstarch and sugar.

3. Cook the sauce on high, stirring often, until it thickens. Add the pineapple and mint and simmer.

4. After the chicken has cooked for 25 minutes, uncover the chicken and drain excess fat.

5. Pour the sauce over the chicken and continue cooking for an additional 10 minutes, or until chicken is cooked thoroughly and begins to brown.

For 2 servings each serving contains				
Calories	503	Fat	2.4g
Protein	41g	Cholesterol	99mg
Carbohydrates	81g	Sodium	114mg

For 3 servings each serving contains				
Calories	335	Fat	1.6g
Protein	27g	Cholesterol	66mg
Carbohydrates	54g	Sodium	76mg

Chicken in Black Bean Sauce ➤

This fragrant dish is a wonderful addition to your cooking repertoire. The sauce is also terrific over rice or seafood. Invite a friend for this classic Cantonese treat. For a chicken entrée, this dish is quite high in carbohydrates as well as protein.

$^1/_2$ cup fermented black beans
$^3/_4$ pound skinless, boneless chicken breast
Paprika
1 onion, minced
2 cloves garlic, minced
2 scallions, chopped
2 teaspoons minced fresh ginger
1 teaspoon vegetable oil
1 ounce shiitake mushrooms, chopped
$^1/_4$ cup chicken stock
$^1/_4$ cup dry sherry or rice wine
2 teaspoons cornstarch dissolved in $^1/_4$ cup cold water
2 tablespoons sugar

1. Rinse the black beans to remove any foreign particles. Cover the beans with cold water and soak until you are ready to use them (at least 15 minutes).

2. Place the chicken in a roasting pan, sprinkle with paprika, and cover. Bake at 400°F for 25 minutes.

3. While the chicken is cooking, sauté the onion, garlic, scallions, and ginger in the oil for 5 minutes over medium heat. Add the chopped shiitake mushrooms and cook for 5 more minutes.

4. Combine the chicken stock, sherry, dissolved cornstarch, and sugar and pour over the onion mixture. Drain the black beans and add to the sauce.

5. Allow the sauce to thicken by increasing the heat, stirring often to prevent sticking.

6. After the chicken has cooked for 25 minutes, uncover it and sprinkle with paprika. Continue cooking the chicken for an additional 10 minutes, or until it is cooked thoroughly and begins to brown. Drain the excess fat. Pour the sauce over the chicken.

For 2 servings
each serving contains

Calories	565	Fat	6g
Protein	53g	Cholesterol	100mg
Carbohydrates	67g	Sodium	1,441mg

For 3 servings
each serving contains

Calories	377	Fat	4g
Protein	35g	Cholesterol	67mg
Carbohydrates	44g	Sodium	961mg

Fesenjen ➤

Fesenjen is a classic Middle Eastern stew. It combines unique flavors like pomegranate and walnuts with onions and chicken. This aromatic dish works well with any meat, from ground beef to wild game. Rabbit and chicken are common choices. This aromatic masterpiece is an excellent source of manganese, magnesium, iron, and fiber.

If you are substituting grenadine for pomegranate juice, note that some brands consist of only red-colored sugar water with flavoring. Check the labels and buy a brand that uses real pomegranate juice.

> ✳ **NOTE** Fruit leather is a pureed fruit that has been dried into a sheet. It is often eaten like candy and can be found in natural food stores as well as your grocery store.

1 1/2 ounces apricot leather, diced (choose an all-natural product when possible)

1 cup water

2 ounces pomegranate juice (or grenadine made with pomegranate juice)

1/8 teaspoon turmeric

1/4 cup tomato paste

1/4 cup dried apricots, chopped, soaked in 1/2 cup boiling water (do not drain)

1/4 cup prunes, chopped, soaked in 1/2 cup boiling water (do not drain)

1/2 teaspoon ground cinnamon

1/8 teaspoon cardamom

1/8 teaspoon ground cloves

1/8 teaspoon ground ginger

1 tablespoon olive oil

1 medium onion, chopped

3/4 pound boneless, skinless chicken breast, cut into 1-inch cubes

1/2 cup walnuts, chopped

3 cups cooked rice

1. Place the apricot leather and water in a saucepan over high heat and bring to a boil. Stir to prevent burning. When the leather begins to soften, after about 5 minutes, add the pomegranate juice, tomato paste, and the dried apricots and prunes with the water they have soaked in. Return to a boil, then reduce heat to low and add the cinnamon, tumeric, cardamom, cloves, and ginger. Set aside.

2. Heat the olive oil in a wok and brown the onion over high heat for about 3 minutes. Add the chicken and continue cooking on high, stirring frequently, until the chicken is cooked on the outside, about 5 minutes. Add the walnuts and continue to cook on high for 2 minutes. Pour the sauce into the wok and simmer for 20 minutes.

3. Serve the stew hot over the rice.

For 2 servings each serving contains	Calories	868	Fat	26g
	Protein	50g	Cholesterol	87mg
	Carbohydrates	113g	Sodium	141mg

For 3 servings each serving contains	Calories	579	Fat	17g
	Protein	33g	Cholesterol	58mg
	Carbohydrates	75g	Sodium	94mg

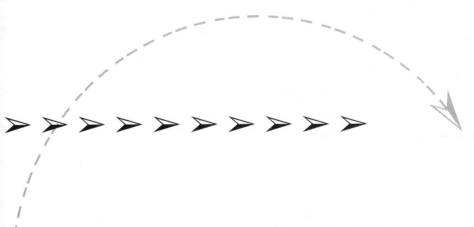

Spicy Pepper Chicken ➤

This Mandarin Chinese dish is high in beta-carotene and is an excellent electrolyte replacer. Match it up with Fried Rice (page 73) and have a great after-workout treat.

1 egg white

1 tablespoon cornstarch

1 tablespoon sherry or rice wine

1 pound skinless, boneless chicken, cut in 1-inch pieces

1¹/₂ cloves garlic, minced

1 tablespoon minced fresh ginger

1 tablespoon vegetable oil

4 ounces frozen vegetables, thawed (we prefer a broccoli and water chestnut mixture)

1 cup fresh mushrooms, sliced

2 scallions, minced

2 hot red peppers, seeded and julienned

¹/₄ green pepper, minced

¹/₂ cup chicken stock

¹/₈ cup soy sauce

1 teaspoon sugar

1. In a bowl, combine the egg white, cornstarch, and sherry. Place the chicken in the bowl with the egg white and coat all of the pieces.

2. In a wok over high heat, sauté the garlic and ginger in the oil for 2 minutes. Do not let the garlic burn. Add the chicken and stir-fry on high until cooked, about 5 minutes. Add the thawed frozen vegetables, mushrooms, scallions, and both kinds of peppers. Cook until heated, about 3 minutes.

3. Add the chicken stock, soy sauce, and sugar to the wok and simmer for 5 minutes more.

For 2 servings
each serving contains

Calories	463	Fat	11g
Protein	60g	Cholesterol	132mg
Carbohydrates	29g	Sodium	1,613mg

For 3 servings
each serving contains

Calories	308	Fat	7g
Protein	40g	Cholesterol	88mg
Carbohydrates	19g	Sodium	1,075mg

Game Hen in Fig Sauce ➤

This dish is a great reflection of the succulent tastes of northern African cuisine. It is high in folic acid as well as beta-carotene. It is also an excellent source of zinc, calcium, and electrolytes.

1 Cornish game hen
Paprika
Salt and freshly ground black pepper

Fig sauce

¹/₄ cup chopped dried figs (about 4)
¹/₈ cup sugar
¹/₈ cup flour
2 tablespoons red wine
1 cup water

Fig couscous

¹/₂ cup fast-cooking couscous
1 clove garlic, minced
³/₄ cup chicken stock
¹/₄ cup chopped dried figs (about 4)

1. Split the game hen in half using a sharp knife. Remove the skin from the bird. Place the halves, bone side down, in a broiler pan. Add paprika, salt, and pepper to taste.

2. Cook the hen under the broiler for 15 minutes, then turn and continue broiling for an additional 10 minutes, or until the hen is cooked.

3. While the hen is cooking, combine ¹/₄ cup figs, sugar, and flour. Add the wine and water to the sauce and cook over high while stirring until the sauce comes to a boil. Reduce heat to medium and continue cooking until the sauce thickens.

4. Combine the fast-cooking couscous with the garlic, stock, and ¹/₄ cup figs. Bring the couscous to a boil in a covered pot, then reduce the heat to low and cook until the water has been absorbed.

5. Spoon the couscous onto a platter and place the game hen on top of it. Pour the fig sauce over the game hen.

For 2 servings each serving contains	Calories	552	Fat	5g
	Protein	43g	Cholesterol	104mg
	Carbohydrates	81g	Sodium	681mg

For 3 servings each serving contains	Calories	368	Fat	4g
	Protein	29g	Cholesterol	69mg
	Carbohydrates	54g	Sodium	454mg

Chicken Pot Pie ➤

A low-fat version of the great American treat. For a quick and novel variation, substitute a can of tuna for the chicken or make this a vegetarian dish without the chicken.

Filling

8 ounces skinless, boneless chicken breast
Salt and freshly ground black pepper
Nonstick vegetable spray
1/4 small onion, minced
4 ounces (1 cup) frozen mixed vegetables, thawed
1/4 green pepper, minced (1/8 cup)
1 cup skim milk
1/2 cup low-sodium chicken stock
1 tablespoon cornstarch dissolved in 1/4 cup cold water

Crust

1 cup whole-wheat flour
1/4 teaspoon salt
3 tablespoons vegetable oil
3 tablespoons cold water

1. Season the chicken breast with salt and pepper, then broil it on both sides until done, about 15 minutes.

2. Meanwhile, heat a nonstick pan over medium-high heat for 30 seconds to 1 minute. Spray with nonstick vegetable spray. Cook the onion, mixed vegetables, and pepper until they begin to soften, about 5 minutes.

3. Combine the skim milk, stock, and dissolved cornstarch in a small pot over medium heat. Bring to a boil, mixing to prevent scorching. Turn the heat to low and add the cooked vegetable mixture. Cut the chicken into 1-inch squares and mix into the vegetables. Continue to simmer the vegetables and chicken on low until you are ready to use.

4. Mix the flour and salt together. Add the oil and blend. Slowly add the cold water, a tablespoon at a time, mixing after each addition.

5. Place the dough in a large plastic bag and roll the crust out until it is flat and about $1/8$- to $1/4$-inch thick.

6. Divide the chicken mixture equally among two 10-ounce or three 8-ounce baking dishes. Tear the plastic bag open and cut the crust to fit the top of each baking dish. Place the crust on top of each dish and bake at 450°F for 15 minutes.

For 2 servings
each serving contains

Calories	643	Fat	21g
Protein	40g	Cholesterol	68mg
Carbohydrates	73g	Sodium	550mg

For 3 servings
each serving contains

Calories	429	Fat	14g
Protein	27g	Cholesterol	45mg
Carbohydrates	49g	Sodium	367mg

Zesty Kabobs ➤

When served with rice, these kabobs are a meal in themselves. They're great before a workout, or on a night when you want to eat lightly. Make the meal special by adding a dessert of vanilla frozen yogurt topped with sliced peaches and drizzled with raspberry liqueur. Cubed swordfish, chuck, or sirloin can be used in place of chicken.

$^1/_2$ cup parboiled brown rice (Minute Rice, Uncle Ben's, etc.) or long-cooking brown rice if you have the time

1 cup water

Marinade

Juice from canned pineapple chunks, about $^3/_4$ cup

$^1/_4$ cup low-salt soy sauce

1 teaspoon grated fresh ginger

2 cloves garlic, chopped

To complete the dish

$^1/_2$ green pepper

$^1/_2$ red pepper

1 onion

$^1/_2$ pound boneless chicken breast, cut in 1-inch cubes (you can buy the chicken already cut for a stir-fry to save time)

15-ounce can pineapple chunks in natural juice

8 cherry tomatoes

8 small skewers

1. Preheat a grill. Begin cooking the rice in the water according to package directions.

2. Mix together all marinade ingredients. Set aside.

3. Cut the peppers and onion into large chunks. Place all the ingredients on skewers, beginning and ending each skewer with a piece of pepper and alternating all other ingredients. Put pineapple next to chicken pieces. Two pieces of chicken should fit on each skewer.

4. Place the skewers in a dish and cover with the marinade. Refrigerate for at least 20 minutes. (You can prepare the recipe up to this point in the morning and let the kabobs marinate in the refrigerator all day.)

5. Cook on a gas grill at medium-high temperature. Drizzle with leftover marinade periodically during cooking, and turn after 5 minutes. Cook for 10 to 15 minutes on a gas grill or until done over charcoal. Kabobs may also be cooked under the broiler following the same directions. Serve over rice.

For 2 servings

Calories	385	Fat	3g
Protein	32g	Cholesterol	66mg
Carbohydrates	58g	Sodium	89mg

For 3 servings

Calories	257	Fat	2g
Protein	21g	Cholesterol	44mg
Carbohydrates	38g	Sodium	60mg

❄ **NOTE** If made with other meat or fish, fat content will be slightly different.

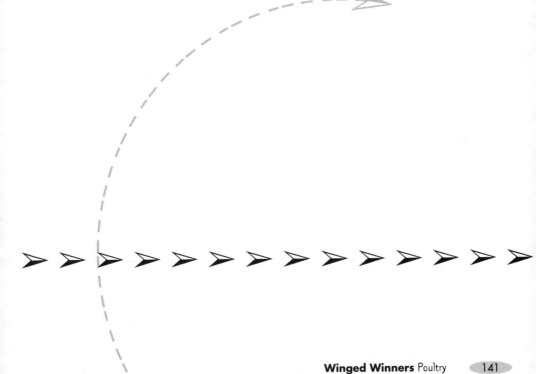

Mandarin Chicken Salad ➤

It is not often that chicken salad is a great source of vitamin C, but this one is. Prepare this light and satisfying salad before a tough workout and come home to a cool, high-energy sandwich.

³/₄ pound skinless, boneless chicken
11-ounce can mandarin oranges, drained
¹/₈ cup chopped pecans
2 stalks celery, chopped
2 hard-boiled egg whites, chopped
2 teaspoons yellow mustard
¹/₈ cup low-fat mayonnaise
¹/₈ cup fat-free yogurt
2 multigrain buns (3 for 3 servings)

1. Place the chicken in a roasting pan and cover it. Bake at 400°F for 25 minutes. Meanwhile, combine the oranges, pecans, celery, and egg whites.

2. When the chicken is cooked, cut into small pieces and toss with the orange mixture. Combine the mustard, mayonnaise, and yogurt and mix into the chicken until all the pieces are well coated.

3. Chill until ready to serve. Fill the rolls with the chicken salad.

For 2 servings
each serving contains

Calories	559	Fat	16g
Protein	51g	Cholesterol	101mg
Carbohydrates	51g	Sodium	748mg

For 3 servings
each serving contains

Calories	393	Fat	11g
Protein	34g	Cholesterol	67mg
Carbohydrates	39g	Sodium	499mg

Curried Chicken Salad ➤

A classic chicken salad with a kick. For a unique presentation, serve in a pineapple shell to create a truly Micronesian sensation.

³/₄ pound skinless, boneless chicken breast
1 tablespoon curry powder
1 cup chicken stock
¹/₂ teaspoon cornstarch dissolved in 2 tablespoons cold water
2 tablespoons nonfat yogurt
1 scallion, minced
¹/₂ cup frozen peas and carrots, thawed

1. Place the chicken in a roasting pan and cover it. Bake at 400°F for 25 minutes.

2. While the chicken is cooking, in a small pot combine the curry powder, stock, and dissolved cornstarch. Cook over high heat while stirring. As soon as the sauce begins to boil, lower the heat and bring the mixture to a simmer. Remove from the heat when it thickens. Add the yogurt to the sauce.

3. When the chicken is cooked, cut into small pieces and combine with the scallion and the peas and carrots. Mix in the sauce and served chilled.

For 2 servings each serving contains				
Calories	269	Fat	4g
Protein	44g	Cholesterol	100mg
Carbohydrates	14g	Sodium	1,470mg

For 3 servings each serving contains				
Calories	180	Fat	3g
Protein	29g	Cholesterol	67mg
Carbohydrates	9g	Sodium	980mg

Turkey Florentine ➤

Ah, Florence! City of Michelangelo's David, and now this elegant city is the inspiration for a low-fat yet spiritual dish. Buono. *An excellent carbohydrates accompaniment to this recipe is Pasta Parmesan (page 61). If you are making more than 1 pound of turkey, add 20 minutes per pound to your cooking time.*

1 pound boned raw turkey breast, sliced about ¹/₄-inch thick
Nonstick vegetable spray
1 tablespoon unsalted butter
1 small onion, diced
1 clove garlic, minced
10-ounce package frozen chopped spinach, thawed
1¹/₂ cups water
2 tablespoons cornstarch dissolved in ¹/₂ cup cold water
¹/₄ cup shredded fat-free mozzarella
¹/₄ cup grated part-skim-milk Parmesan

1. Stack the slices of turkey and place in a baking dish coated with nonstick vegetable spray. Cover with aluminum foil and bake at 400°F for 20 minutes.

2. While the turkey is cooking, sauté the onion and garlic in the butter for 5 minutes over medium heat. Add the spinach. Add the water and the cornstarch mixture and stir while bringing the water to a boil. Continue stirring until the mixture thickens. Reduce the heat to low.

3. Uncover the turkey and continue to bake it until it is cooked, about 10 minutes more. Remove the turkey from the pan and drain any fat from the pan. Separate the turkey slices with a fork and place half of the turkey in a single layer back in the pan. Spoon the spinach over the turkey and place the rest of the turkey over the spinach.

4. Sprinkle with fat-free shredded mozzarella and Parmesan cheese. Place under the broiler until the cheese melts. Serve immediately.

For 2 servings
each serving contains

Calories	514	Fat	15g
Protein	55g	Cholesterol	148mg
Carbohydrates	39g	Sodium	2,054mg

For 3 servings
each serving contains

Calories	343	Fat	10g
Protein	36g	Cholesterol	98mg
Carbohydrates	26g	Sodium	1,369mg

Baked Turkey in Plum Sauce ➤

This recipe is high in simple sugar, so if the plums are sweet reduce the sugar to taste. This recipe goes very well with Praline Sweet Potatoes (page 68). If you are making more than 1 pound of turkey, add 20 minutes per pound to your cooking time. Remember, plums are just prunes with better complexions; they're high in chromium and fiber, too.

1 pound boned, sliced raw turkey breast
Nonstick vegetable spray
6 plums, pitted and diced
1 cup sugar
1 cup water

1. Stack the slices of turkey and place in a pan coated with nonstick vegetable spray. Cover with aluminum foil and bake at 400°F for 20 minutes.

2. While the turkey is cooking, combine the diced plums and water in a small pot. Bring the water to a boil, then reduce heat and simmer until the plums are tender. Add the sugar and continue to cook until the sugar is dissolved.

3. Uncover the turkey and continue to bake it until it is cooked, about 10 minutes. Separate the turkey slices with a fork and place on a platter. Pour the plum sauce over the turkey.

For 2 servings
each serving contains

Calories	766	Fat	6g
Protein	42g	Cholesterol	120mg
Carbohydrates	140g	Sodium	941mg

For 3 servings
each serving contains

Calories	511	Fat	4g
Protein	28g	Cholesterol	80mg
Carbohydrates	93g	Sodium	628mg

Turkey-stuffed Eggplant ➢

Dishes made with stuffed vegetables like peppers and cabbage are common in Eastern Europe. Our version uses an eggplant and a slightly sweet low-fat filling.

1 eggplant (about 1 pound)
¹/₃ cup catsup
1 tablespoon brown mustard
1 tablespoon lemon juice
2 tablespoons brown sugar
¹/₂ cup whole-wheat flour
¹/₂ pound ground turkey
Salt and freshly ground black pepper

1. With a fork pierce a number of holes in the eggplant. Microwave the eggplant on high for 2 minutes. Turn the eggplant over and microwave for an additional 3 minutes. (To cook the eggplant conventionally, cut it lengthwise and steam in a large pot for 10 to 15 minutes, until tender.)

2. Combine the catsup, mustard, lemon juice, and brown sugar. Add the flour and turkey and mix thoroughly.

3. Slice the eggplant in half and scoop out the inside, leaving a ¹/₄-inch layer of eggplant intact. Mash the eggplant and add a small amount of salt and freshly ground black pepper to taste.

4. Put half of the mashed eggplant back into each half of the eggplant shell. Place half of the ground turkey mixture on top of the mashed eggplant in each eggplant shell.

5. Microwave the eggplant on high for 5 minutes. Place the eggplant under the broiler for an additional 5 minutes, or until the turkey begins to brown. (If you want to cook it conventionally, cook in a hot oven, on the bottom shelf, for about 15 minutes.)

For 2 servings	Calories	401	Fat	4g
each serving contains	Protein	28g	Cholesterol	60mg
	Carbohydrates	69g	Sodium	1,378mg

For 3 servings	Calories	267	Fat	3g
each serving contains	Protein	18g	Cholesterol	40mg
	Carbohydrates	46g	Sodium	919mg

✴ **NOTE** To reduce the sodium, use low-sodium catsup.

Turkey Joes ➤

This variation on the classic sloppy joe can be enjoyed by anyone on a high-performance diet. Using turkey instead of beef lowers the fat content to acceptable levels. Turkey is also a good source of iron.

1 onion, diced
¹/₄ sweet green pepper, diced
1 teaspoon oil
³/₄ pound ground turkey
1 tablespoon fresh oregano
1 tablespoon fresh basil
1 teaspoon crushed bay leaf
12-ounce can tomato paste
¹/₂ cup water
2 multigrain buns or hamburger buns (3 for 3 servings)

1. Sauté the onion and green pepper in the oil for 5 minutes over medium heat. Add the turkey and cook thoroughly, about 10 minutes. If the turkey begins to stick to the pan, add a small amount of water (¹/₄ cup).

2. Add the oregano, basil, bay leaf, and tomato paste and slowly add enough water so that the mixture is smooth but not runny. You do not have to use all the water. Simmer for 5 minutes.

3. Serve on buns.

For 2 servings each serving contains				
Calories	657	Fat	11g
Protein	48g	Cholesterol	93mg
Carbohydrates	103g	Sodium	1,832mg

For 3 servings each serving contains				
Calories	523	Fat	8g
Protein	35g	Cholesterol	63mg
Carbohydrates	86g	Sodium	1,409mg

Turkey Chili ➤

This is the perfect meal to follow winter sports: A hearty blend of aromatic spices combines with the bite of chilies to guarantee a stick-to-your-ribs experience. Just add a great bread. If you want to reduce the sodium in this recipe, use low-sodium chicken bouillon and "no salt added" canned tomatoes.

3 cardamom seeds
1¹/₂ teaspoons cumin seed
1 teaspoon cinnamon
1 teaspoon unsweetened cocoa
2¹/₂ teaspoons chili powder
1 teaspoon marjoram
2 teaspoons dried chicken bouillon
1 onion, sliced
1 teaspoon garlic, minced
1 teaspoon extra-virgin olive oil
³/₄ pound ground turkey
2 hot chili peppers
¹/₄ cup sherry
¹/₂ cup water
28-ounce can whole tomatoes, drained

1. Put the cardamom seeds and cumin seeds in a small, microwave-safe bowl and heat for 30 seconds, or toast in a frying pan over medium-high heat. Grind the heated seeds in a spice mill or food processor and combine with the cinnamon, cocoa, chili powder, marjoram, and chicken bouillon.

2. Sauté the onion and garlic over low heat in the oil. When the onion is tender, after about 5 minutes, add the ground turkey and cook until it browns, about 5 minutes.

3. Slice the chili peppers and remove the seeds. For a milder chili use only 1 pepper. Wash your hands thoroughly after cutting the chili peppers, before touching your face or eyes.

4. Add the spice mixture, chilies, sherry, water, and tomatoes to the turkey. Allow to simmer for an additional 10 minutes.

For 2 servings	Calories	432	Fat	9g
each serving contains	Protein	37g	Cholesterol	93mg
	Carbohydrates	49g	Sodium	2,965mg

For 3 servings	Calories	288	Fat	6g
each serving contains	Protein	25g	Cholesterol	62mg
	Carbohydrates	33g	Sodium	1,977mg

Turkey Bolognese ➤

Experts consider Bologna to be the Italian city with the most inspired cuisine. After tasting this delicato blend of mushrooms and tomatoes, you'll agree. Of course, this recipe is unique because of the nontraditional use of turkey.

1 clove garlic, minced
1 tablespoon extra-virgin olive oil
3/4 pound turkey breast, pounded and cubed
2 tomatoes, diced
2 ounces mushrooms, sliced
1/4 cup balsamic vinegar
1/4 cup red wine
1 bunch (20 sprigs) fresh parsley, chopped
6 ounces dried pasta, cooked according to package directions

1. Sauté the garlic in the olive oil over medium heat for 30 seconds. Add the turkey cubes and brown for 5 minutes.

2. Add the diced tomatoes, mushrooms, vinegar, and wine to the turkey. Simmer for 10 minutes. Add the chopped parsley, mix thoroughly, and serve immediately over the pasta.

For 2 servings	Calories	562	Fat	10g
each serving contains	Protein	54g	Cholesterol	168mg
	Carbohydrates	58g	Sodium	126mg

For 3 servings	Calories	375	Fat	7g
each serving contains	Protein	36g	Cholesterol	112mg
	Carbohydrates	38g	Sodium	84mg

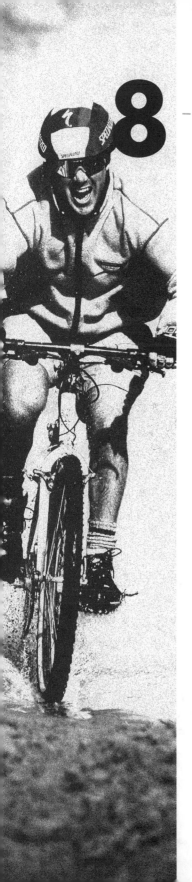

8

Blue-Ribbon BEASTS Beef, Pork, and Lamb

Magnificent Moussaka ➤

*While traveling through Greece, I thoroughly enjoyed the array of new
and fresh vegetables used in the national cuisine. One of the most popular
vegetables is eggplant, and moussaka was my favorite dish. Prepared in
the traditional way, moussaka is very high in fat and calories. This recipe
is a fabulous healthful rendition that you can enjoy regularly. (SMK)*

1 small eggplant (about ³/₄ pound)
Nonstick cooking spray
1 teaspoon garlic powder
¹/₂ pound extra-lean ground round
1 small onion, chopped
¹/₂ cup dry white wine
4 ounces no-salt-added tomato sauce
1 tablespoon minced fresh parsley
¹/₄ teaspoon black pepper
Pinch ground nutmeg
2 tablespoons all-purpose unbleached flour
Pinch white pepper
¹/₂ can (6 ounces) evaporated skim milk
2 ounces low-sodium chicken broth
2 tablespoons grated Parmesan cheese

1. Preheat oven to 425°F. Cut the eggplant into ¹/₄-inch slices. Arrange the eggplant slices in a single layer on a nonstick baking sheet and coat the top surface of the eggplant with cooking spray. Sprinkle with garlic powder and bake in oven for 15 minutes, or until lightly browned. Set aside.

2. While eggplant is cooking, combine the ground round and onion in a large nonstick skillet and cook over medium heat until browned, about 10 minutes, stirring to crumble.

3. Once the meat has browned, add the wine, tomato sauce, parsley, black pepper, and nutmeg. Cook for 15 minutes, stirring occasionally. Remove from the heat and cool.

4. In a small bowl, mix the flour and white pepper. Put the milk in a medium saucepan over medium heat and whisk in flour mixture. Add chicken broth. Heat 5 to 7 minutes, stirring frequently, until thickened.

5. In a 1-quart microwave-safe dish, arrange $^1/_3$ of the eggplant and top with $^1/_3$ of the meat mixture. Spread $^1/_3$ of the white sauce over meat and top with $^1/_3$ of the Parmesan cheese. Repeat twice more with remaining eggplant, meat mixture, white sauce, and cheese. Cover and warm in microwave at 50% power for 5 minutes, or until moussaka is thoroughly heated. (You can also cook in a 350°F oven for 30 minutes.)

For 2 servings
each serving contains

Calories	462	Fat	14g
Protein	36g	Cholesterol	76mg
Carbohydrates	40g	Sodium	359mg

For 3 servings
each serving contains

Calories	308	Fat	9g
Protein	24g	Cholesterol	51mg
Carbohydrates	27g	Sodium	240mg

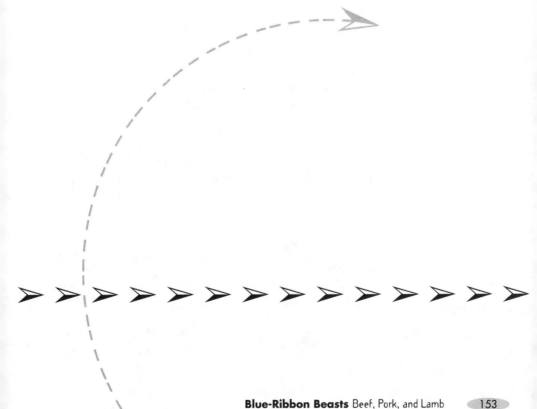

Blue Sky Chili ➤

This is one of our favorite beef dishes. A hefty meal, it is a real treat after a long winter hike in the woods. The beef will boost your iron stores, and the beans will keep your cholesterol down.

1/2 pound extra-lean ground round
1/4 cup chopped celery
1 small onion, chopped
1 small green pepper, chopped
1/2 teaspoon canola oil
1 clove garlic, minced
1/4 cup water
2 1/2 tablespoons chili powder
1/2 tablespoon cumin
10 ounces (1 1/4 cups) chopped tomatoes
10 ounces (1 1/4 cups) low-salt strained or puréed tomatoes
1/4 teaspoon dried oregano
1/4 teaspoon sugar
15-ounce can kidney beans, drained
1/2 tablespoon jarred green chili peppers, minced

1. Brown the meat in a skillet over medium heat for about 10 minutes, breaking into small pieces.

2. At the same time, in a nonstick skillet, sauté the celery, onion, and green pepper in the oil over medium-high heat for 5 minutes.

3. Combine the cooked meat and vegetables in a large pot. Add the garlic. Mix together the water, chili powder, and cumin and add to the meat mixture. Add both types of canned tomatoes, oregano, and sugar. Bring the mixture to a boil. Reduce the heat to low and simmer, covered, for 15 minutes. Stir to prevent sticking. Uncover and simmer an additional 15 minutes.

4. During the last 15 minutes of cooking, add the beans and chili peppers.

For 2 servings each serving contains	Calories	536	Fat	16g
	Protein	38g	Cholesterol	69mg
	Carbohydrates	68g	Sodium	1,336mg

For 3 servings each serving contains	Calories	357	Fat	11g
	Protein	25g	Cholesterol	46mg
	Carbohydrates	45g	Sodium	890mg

Beef Fajita ➤

In San Antonio the saying goes, "Remember the Alamo." The fact that San Antonio gave us a tasty use for low-fat flank steak is also worth remembering. This is an excellent source of iron.

Juice from **1** lime
¹/₄ cup beer
2 drops Tabasco (optional)
¹/₂ pound flank steak, thinly sliced
Nonstick vegetable spray
1 onion, sliced
1 green pepper, sliced
1 tomato, sliced
2 tortillas (3 for 3 servings)
Salsa (page 52)
2 tablespoons fat-free sour cream

1. Combine the lime juice, beer, and Tabasco. Marinate the flank steak in the mixture for at least 20 minutes and as long as overnight, covered and refrigerated.

2. Spray an oven-safe skillet with nonstick vegetable spray and heat under the broiler for 4 minutes. Place the flank steak, onion, green pepper, and tomato in the pan and broil for 5 minutes. Turn the meat and vegetables over for even cooking and brush with the marinade. Cook for an additional 5 minutes, or until done. Discard the extra marinade.

3. Wet 2 paper towels and wrap them around the tortillas. Place in the microwave and heat for 1 minute, or until warm.

4. Assemble the fajita by placing the meat and vegetables in the tortillas and rolling the tortillas up. Garnish with salsa and sour cream.

For 2 servings each serving contains				
Calories	429	Fat	12g
Protein	42g	Cholesterol	100mg
Carbohydrates	39g	Sodium	95mg

For 3 servings each serving contains				
Calories	264	Fat	8g
Protein	27g	Cholesterol	66mg
Carbohydrates	22g	Sodium	63mg

Grilled Steak Sandwich ➤

A little red meat goes a long way to satisfy your taste buds and boost your iron stores. Our variation of the marinade on this steak sandwich has more to do with Florence, Italy, than with South Philadelphia, but as Rocky says. . . . Yo, steak!

¹/₈ cup balsamic vinegar

¹/₈ cup dry red wine

1 teaspoon minced garlic

¹/₈ teaspoon black pepper

¹/₂ pound butt steak, trimmed of fat, sliced into 2 steaks (3 steaks for 3 servings)

2 slices ripe red tomato (3 for 3 servings)

2 slices yellow onion (3 for 3 servings)

2 lettuce leaves, any variety (3 for 3 servings)

2 multigrain buns (3 for 3 servings)

1. Combine the vinegar, wine, garlic, and pepper. Marinate the butt steaks in the marinade for at least 10 minutes or as long as overnight, covered and refrigerated.

2. Broil the butt steaks for 5 minutes on each side or until done to your liking. Place the tomato, onion, lettuce, and meat on multigrain buns and serve immediately.

For 2 servings each serving contains	Calories	459	Fat	11g
	Protein	34g	Cholesterol	70mg
	Carbohydrates	58g	Sodium	643mg

For 3 servings each serving contains	Calories	395	Fat	8g
	Protein	26g	Cholesterol	48mg
	Carbohydrates	37g	Sodium	617mg

Retro Meatloaf ➤

This 1950s favorite is making a low-fat return.

4 slices fat-free bread, toasted
7 ounces lean ground beef
1 shallot, minced
1 egg white
Salt and freshly ground black pepper
1 tomato, sliced
¹/₄ cup favorite barbecue sauce, or see recipe on page 129.
2 multigrain buns (3 for 3 servings)

1. Put the toasted bread in a blender or food processor and blend until crumbed. Combine the bread crumbs, ground beef, shallot, egg white, salt, and freshly ground black pepper. Form the beef mixture into 2 or 3 patties and place on the grill or under the broiler.

2. Cook for 4 to 6 minutes, then turn. Brush with barbecue sauce and add the sliced tomato. Continue cooking until done, about 3 minutes. Place on buns and serve.

For 2 servings each serving contains	Calories	748	Fat	23g
	Protein	40g	Cholesterol	82mg
	Carbohydrates	97g	Sodium	1,281mg

For 3 servings each serving contains	Calories	584	Fat	17g
	Protein	30g	Cholesterol	55mg
	Carbohydrates	82g	Sodium	1,042mg

Lean and Mean Pork Tenderloin ➤

Many people still believe that pork is high in fat. On the contrary, the present style of raising pork produces a lean animal with little marbling in the meat. The tenderloin is especially lean and delicious, and it cooks very quickly. This recipe includes one of our favorite sauces for pork. Hoisin sauce, five-spice powder, and candied ginger should be available in your local supermarket.

1 tablespoon plus 1 teaspoon hoisin sauce

1/3 teaspoon five-spice powder

1/2 clove garlic, minced

1 teaspoon coarsely shredded fresh ginger

1 tablespoon plus 1 teaspoon white wine

1/2 pound whole pork tenderloin

1 cup plus 1 tablespoon water

3 teaspoons chopped candied ginger

1/2 cup parboiled enriched white rice

1. Mix the hoisin, five-spice powder, garlic, ginger, and wine in a bowl large enough to hold the pork.

2. Wash and dry the pork and marinate it for at least 20 minutes or up to a full day, covered and refrigerated. Remove the pork from the marinade and separate the thinner part of the tenderloin. Reserve the marinade.

3. Heat the broiler or stovetop grill and cook both pieces of tenderloin, allowing 12 to 15 minutes for the thicker part and a little less for the thinner.

4. Boil 1 cup of water for the rice. Once the water is boiling, add 2 teaspoons candied ginger and the rice, reduce the heat to low, and cover. Cook until done, about 15 minutes.

5. While the rice is cooking, mix in the remaining teaspoon of candied ginger and 1 tablespoon of water to the marinade. (Slightly more water can be added if necessary.) Place in a small, microwave-safe container and reheat to a boil, about 1 minute.

6. Slice the meat and spoon the marinade over it. Serve with rice.

For 2 servings
each serving contains

Calories	344	Fat	3g
Protein	27g	Cholesterol	74mg
Carbohydrates	48g	Sodium	117mg

For 3 servings
each serving contains

Calories	230	Fat	2g
Protein	18g	Cholesterol	49mg
Carbohydrates	32g	Sodium	78mg

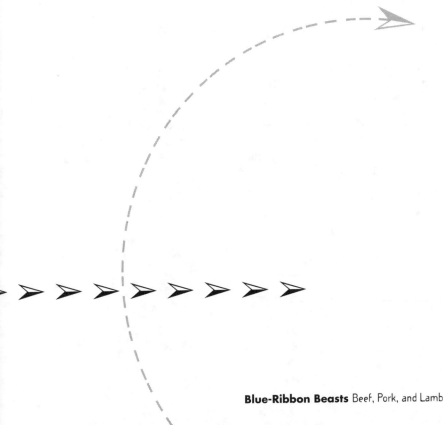

Sweet Taste of Summer Pork ➤

Pork is an excellent source of thiamin, a vitamin critically linked to energy production. Having cherries to cook with in the middle of winter has become a great treat. Dried cherries are usually found in the dried fruit section of the supermarket.

¹/₂ cup (4 ounces) low-salt chicken broth
3 tablespoons brandy
3¹/₂ tablespoons dried tart cherries
¹/₈ teaspoon dried thyme
Pinch ground allspice
¹/₂ pound pork tenderloin, cut into 1-inch-thick slices
2 teaspoons unsalted butter
1 shallot, minced
3 tablespoons evaporated skim milk
Salt and freshly ground black pepper

1. Combine the chicken broth, brandy, cherries, thyme, and allspice in a small, heavy saucepan. Cover and simmer over low heat until the cherries are plump and tender, about 10 minutes.

2. Place the pork between two sheets of plastic wrap and pound until ¹/₂-inch thick.

3. Melt the butter in a large, heavy skillet over medium-high heat. Season the pork with a little salt and freshly ground black pepper and cook until just brown, about 1¹/₂ minutes per side. Transfer the pork to a plate.

4. Add the minced shallot to the skillet and stir for 30 seconds. Stir in the cherry mixture and bring to a boil. Add the milk and simmer until the mixture reduces to a saucelike consistency, about 4 minutes. Season the sauce lightly with salt and freshly ground black pepper.

5. Return the pork and any juices on the plate to the skillet. Simmer until the pork is cooked through, about 1 minute. Transfer to a platter and serve.

For 2 servings each serving contains	Calories	249	Fat	7g
	Protein	27g	Cholesterol	85mg
	Carbohydrates	12g	Sodium	317mg

For 3 servings each serving contains	Calories	166	Fat	5g
	Protein	18g	Cholesterol	57mg
	Carbohydrates	8g	Sodium	211mg

The Pork and Mustard Caper ➤

For some really lean and tender meat, try this easy recipe. This low-fat entrée is high in iron, thiamin, and vitamin B-12.

1 cup water
1/4 cup apple juice
2 teaspoons dry white wine
1 clove garlic, chopped
2 teaspoons prepared yellow mustard
1 tablespoon lemon juice
1 teaspoon sugar
1 teaspoon Worcestershire sauce
2 tablespoons capers
Nonstick cooking spray
1/2 pound pork tenderloin, cut into 1/4-inch slices
1 teaspoon cornstarch dissolved in 2 tablespoons cold water

1. Mix together the water, apple juice, wine, garlic, mustard, lemon juice, sugar, Worcestershire sauce, and capers.

2. Heat a nonstick skillet over high heat for seconds. Spray with nonstick cooking spray and add the pork. Quickly brown the pork, cooking for about 3 minutes. Add the combined liquid ingredients. Bring to a simmer over low heat just until the pork is done. Remove the pork to a serving plate.

3. Raise the heat and cook the liquid in the pan until reduced, about 5 minutes. Stir in the dissolved cornstarch and heat until slightly thickened.

4. Return the pork to the sauce, with any juices, just until the pork is heated through. Serve immediately.

For 2 servings each serving contains				
Calories	170	Fat	3g
Protein	24g	Cholesterol	74mg
Carbohydrates	9g	Sodium	122mg

For 3 servings each serving contains				
Calories	113	Fat	2g
Protein	16g	Cholesterol	49mg
Carbohydrates	6g	Sodium	81mg

Glazed Ham with Raisin-Apricot Sauce ➤

Glazed ham is not just a holiday meal anymore. With its California fruits, high electrolytes, and low fat content, this recipe makes a great after-workout meal.

¹/₄ cup fresh orange juice
¹/₂ tablespoon honey
¹/₄ teaspoon prepared yellow mustard
¹/₄ teaspoon soy sauce
¹/₂ pound center-cut ham steak (³/₄-inch thick)

Sauce

¹/₂ tablespoon sugar
¹/₂ tablespoon cornstarch
¹/₂ tablespoon unsalted butter
¹/₄ teaspoon cinnamon
¹/₈ teaspoon ginger
1 cup fresh orange juice
¹/₂ cup raisins
7 dried apricots, chopped (about ¹/₄ cup)

1. Combine the ¹/₄ cup orange juice, honey, mustard, and soy sauce. Brush the ham with the glaze and broil for 15 minutes, glazed side up. Turn the ham over, brush with more glaze, and cook for an additional 15 minutes. While it's cooking, continue to brush with glaze to prevent it from drying out.

2. Meanwhile, combine the sugar, cornstarch, and butter in a small pot. Heat over medium while mixing until all ingredients are blended. Add the cinnamon, ginger, and 1 cup orange juice to the pot. Increase the heat to high and continue mixing until the sauce begins to boil. Reduce the heat to low and add the raisins and apricots. Place the ham on a platter and pour the sauce over it.

For 2 servings each serving contains	Calories	422	Fat	9g
	Protein	26g	Cholesterol	59mg
	Carbohydrates	65g	Sodium	1,489mg

For 3 servings each serving contains	Calories	281	Fat	6g
	Protein	17g	Cholesterol	39mg
	Carbohydrates	44g	Sodium	993mg

Glazed Grilled Lamb Chops ➤

*It's glazed, it's grilled, it's delicious. The process of grilling can help reduce
your fat intake. Always make sure to trim extra fat, and avoid cooking too close
to the hot coals to minimize the possibility of producing nitrosamines, which are
cancer-causing agents. This recipe also works well with other chops, like pork.*

¹/₂ cup honey

2 tablespoons low-sodium soy sauce

1 tablespoon lemon juice

3 cloves garlic, minced

1 pound lamb chops with bone, trimmed of fat

Nonstick vegetable spray

7 medium mushrooms, sliced

4 ounces fresh or frozen broccoli florets

1 cup water

1 teaspoon cornstarch dissolved in ¹/₄ cup cold water

6 ounces dried rotini, cooked according to package directions

1. Combine the honey, soy sauce, lemon juice, and garlic. Mix well. Brush both
   sides of the lamb with honey sauce and place on the grill to cook. Grill on
   both sides to desired doneness.

2. Meanwhile, spray a nonstick frying pan with nonstick vegetable spray and
   sauté the mushrooms and broccoli on medium heat until they begin to soften.
   Add the remaining honey sauce to the vegetables along with the water and
   dissolved cornstarch. When sauce has thickened, place the lamb on a bed of
   rotini and pour the honey glaze over it. Serve immediately.

For 2 servings each serving contains				
Calories	848	Fat	18g
Protein	48g	Cholesterol	174mg
Carbohydrates	128g	Sodium	1,199mg

For 3 servings each serving contains				
Calories	565	Fat	12g
Protein	32g	Cholesterol	116mg
Carbohydrates	85g	Sodium	799mg

Shashlik with Pepper Rice ➤

For the uninitiated, this is a Middle Eastern lamb kabob, not the sound of a sneeze. This dish makes it easy to eat four out of six food groups in one fell swoop.

¹/₈ cup lemon juice

¹/₈ cup dry red wine

¹/₈ cup extra virgin olive oil

1 teaspoon dried rosemary

1 teaspoon minced garlic

¹/₄ teaspoon crushed red pepper

¹/₂ teaspoon salt

¹/₈ teaspoon freshly ground black pepper

1 pound lean lamb, trimmed of fat and cut into 1-inch cubes

4 mushrooms, halved

1 small yellow summer squash, cut into 1-inch slices

¹/₂ sweet red bell pepper, cut into 1-inch squares

2 small onions, halved

4 metal skewers or wood skewers (soaked in water for 1 hour so they won't burn)

Pepper Rice

1 cup beef stock

1 cup water

¹/₂ sweet red bell pepper, minced

2 cups 10-minute brown rice

1. Combine the lemon juice, wine, oil, rosemary, garlic, crushed red pepper, salt, and black pepper in a bowl. Add the lamb cubes and marinate for at least 10 minutes or as long as overnight, covered and refrigerated.

2. Place a piece of one of the vegetables on a skewer, followed by a piece of meat, and alternate the vegetables and meat until all four skewers are filled. Brush the extra marinade over the vegetables on the skewers.

3. Spray a broiler pan with nonstick vegetable spray, place the shashlik in the pan, and broil for 10 minutes, turning for even browning. Or cook outside on the grill for the same time. Continue to brush the shashlik with the marinade as it cooks to prevent drying. Dispose of any extra marinade; do not serve it.

4. Meanwhile, bring the beef stock and water to a boil and add the red pepper and brown rice. Cover the pot and reduce the heat to low. Allow to simmer for 10 minutes. Place the cooked rice on a platter and serve the shashlik on top.

For 2 servings
each serving contains

Calories	451	Fat	8g
Protein	36g	Cholesterol	74mg
Carbohydrates	56g	Sodium	1,268mg

For 3 servings
each serving contains

Calories	301	Fat	6g
Protein	24g	Cholesterol	49mg
Carbohydrates	38g	Sodium	845mg

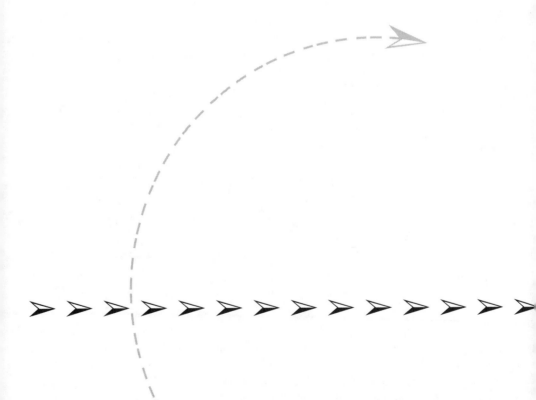

9

Backpack
SNACKS
Snacks and
Traveling
Recipes

Trail Mix ➤

This is a heavy-duty trail mix that is truly great in the outdoors when you are very active. It's high in calories and can handle the heat.

4 ounces minipretzels
2¹/₂ ounces honey-roasted dry-roasted peanuts
2 ounces dried cherries
1 ounce dried blueberries

1. Mix all the ingredients in a plastic bag and enjoy on the trail.

For 2 servings
each serving contains

Calories	625	Fat	22g
Protein	17g	Cholesterol	0mg
Carbohydrates	99g	Sodium	1,075mg

For 3 servings
each serving contains

Calories	417	Fat	14g
Protein	11g	Cholesterol	0mg
Carbohydrates	66g	Sodium	718mg

Spaghetti Cakes ➤

This high-carbohydrate treat is a great snack hot or cold. It is based on the noodle kugels prepared by eastern European Jews. We have substituted spaghetti for egg noodles to reduce the cholesterol.

6 ounces dried spaghetti, cooked (do not rinse)
2 eggs, beaten
¹/₂ cup raisins
¹/₄ cup fruit preserves
1 teaspoon cinnamon
1 teaspoon unsalted butter, melted
Nonstick vegetable spray

1. Combine the cooked spaghetti, eggs, raisins, fruit preserves, cinnamon, and butter.

2. Spray a nonstick cupcake tin with nonstick vegetable spray. Divide the spaghetti mixture evenly to make 6 cupcakes.

3. Bake at 350°F for 25 minutes, or until the tops are golden brown and crusty.

For 2 servings each serving contains	Calories	623	Fat	9g
	Protein	18g	Cholesterol	218mg
	Carbohydrates	121g	Sodium	100mg

For 3 servings each serving contains	Calories	415	Fat	6g
	Protein	12g	Cholesterol	145mg
	Carbohydrates	80g	Sodium	66mg

Bagel Chips with Garlic ➤

These are an excellent replacement for potato chips, and they pack well for travel.

2 bagels
4 cloves garlic, peeled
1 tablespoon pure olive oil

1. Slice the bagels in half. Slice each half in half again, to form large round chips.

2. Microwave the garlic on low for 2 minutes. Press the garlic through a garlic press. Combine with the olive oil to make a paste.

3. Spread the paste on the bagels and toast until light brown. Serve immediately, or store in a plastic bag for snacking.

For 2 servings each serving contains	Calories	269	Fat	9g
	Protein	7g	Cholesterol	0mg
	Carbohydrates	40g	Sodium	246mg

For 3 servings each serving contains	Calories	179	Fat	6g
	Protein	5g	Cholesterol	0mg
	Carbohydrates	27g	Sodium	164mg

Vegetable Cheese Rolls ➤

This low-fat treat is a wonderful source of carbohydrates. The rolls can also be made with other cheeses and vegetables, so start experimenting! (We use Pillsbury Crusty French Bread dough.)

2 scallions, chopped
2 ounces fat-free mozzarella, shredded
1 unbaked loaf French or Italian refrigerator dough

1. Unroll the dough to form a flat sheet. Sprinkle the shredded cheese and scallions onto the dough. Roll the dough back up to form a loaf.

2. Divide the dough into 2 equal balls (3 for 3 servings) and place on a nonstick cookie sheet. Bake at 350°F for 15 to 20 minutes, or until brown. The rolls can be eaten immediately or taken on the road.

For 2 servings
each serving contains

Calories	416	Fat	3g
Protein	24g	Cholesterol	5mg
Carbohydrates	71g	Sodium	1,125mg

For 3 servings
each serving contains

Calories	277	Fat	2g
Protein	16g	Cholesterol	3mg
Carbohydrates	47g	Sodium	750mg

Cinnamon Raisin Rolls ➤

This low-fat sweet treat will remind you of the sweet smells of your local bakery, and it is a lot of fun to make. The trick lies in spreading the applesauce mixture in a thin layer so that pockets of apple do not cause the dough to fall apart. (We use Pillsbury Crusty French Bread dough.) You can add pecans to this for pecan rolls, but it will increase the fat. We often mix ¹/₈ cup of powdered (confectioners') sugar and a few drops of hot water to form a glaze for the tops of the rolls.

¹/₄ cup brown sugar

1 teaspoon cinnamon

¹/₈ cup applesauce

1 unbaked loaf French or Italian refrigerator dough

¹/₄ cup raisins

1. Mix the brown sugar, cinnamon, and applesauce together. Unroll the dough and form a flat sheet. Spread the applesauce mixture onto the dough. Sprinkle with the raisins.

2. Divide the dough into 2 equal balls (3 for 3 servings) and place on a nonstick cookie sheet. Bake at 350°F for 15 to 20 minutes, or until brown. The rolls can be eaten hot or cold.

For 2 servings
each serving contains

Calories	506	Fat	3g
Protein	16g	Cholesterol	0mg
Carbohydrates	104g	Sodium	933mg

For 3 servings
each serving contains

Calories	337	Fat	2g
Protein	10g	Cholesterol	0mg
Carbohydrates	70g	Sodium	622mg

Caramel Corn ➤

A classic crunchy, high-fiber treat. You can eat it immediately and have sticky fingers, or let it sit for three or four hours until it dries.

1 envelope low-fat microwave popcorn
15 caramel candies
2 tablespoons skim milk

1. Microwave the popcorn according to package directions. Allow to cool in a large bowl.

2. Microwave the caramel candy and milk on high for 2 minutes. Stir and repeat until a sauce has formed. Pour over the popcorn and toss until all the popcorn has been coated. The caramel corn will start out sticky but will slowly get drier.

For 2 servings
each serving contains

Calories	319	Fat	8g
Protein	4g	Cholesterol	2mg
Carbohydrates	61g	Sodium	321mg

For 3 servings
each serving contains

Calories	213	Fat	5g
Protein	3g	Cholesterol	1mg
Carbohydrates	41g	Sodium	214mg

Oatmeal Chewies ➤

These very low-fat, high-fiber treats are chewy rather than crisp. If you prefer a harder cookie, leave them out overnight.

1¹/₄ cups applesauce

1 cup brown sugar

1 egg, beaten

1 teaspoon vanilla

1¹/₂ cups flour

1 teaspoon baking soda

1 teaspoon cinnamon

3 cups uncooked oatmeal

¹/₂ cup raisins

1. Combine the applesauce, sugar, egg, and vanilla. Mix well. Add the flour, baking soda, cinnamon, oatmeal, and raisins. Stir until all ingredients are combined.

2. Drop the batter onto a nonstick cookie sheet with a tablespoon. Bake at 375°F for 8 to 10 minutes. Makes about 16 cookies.

For 8 servings each serving contains

Calories	434	Fat	5g
Protein	13g	Cholesterol	27mg
Carbohydrates	86g	Sodium	105mg

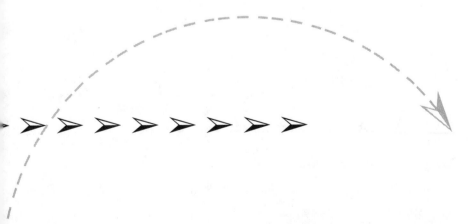

Nutty Fruit Balls (Haroseth) ➤

Many people eat this as a dessert or snack throughout the year. Its origins are Middle Eastern, and is part of the Sephardic Passover seder. It is an excellent source of trace elements such as manganese and magnesium.

10 dried figlets or **5** dried large figs (stems removed)
¹/₂ cup (about 10 halves) dried apricots
³/₄ cup water
³/₄ ounce dried, unsalted almonds (about 11)
1 ounce hazelnuts (about 15), ground

1. Place the figs, apricots, and water in a dish and microwave on high for 5 minutes.

2. Place the fruit and water in a food processor and purée for 3 minutes. Add the almonds and purée for an additional 1 minute. Some almond chunks should remain.

3. Place the ground hazelnuts in a bowl. With a teaspoon, drop small balls of the fruit mixture into the hazelnuts and coat the outside. Place on waxed paper and refrigerate until set, about 1 hour. Makes 8 balls.

For 4 servings
each serving contains

Calories	246	Fat	8g
Protein	4g	Cholesterol	0mg
Carbohydrates	46g	Sodium	8mg

10

Photo
FINISHES
Desserts

Sorbet

Making sorbet is really an activity unto itself. Sorbets come out best when you use an ice-cream maker and freeze the mixtures according to the manufacturer's directions. We always prechill the mixture in the freezer before putting it in the ice-cream maker to ensure a well-frozen product. Don't let the mixture freeze when you are prechilling it.

You can also freeze the mixture to a frozen slush in ice cube trays (small pans are easier to dump into your blender but take much longer to freeze), then purée the cubes in a blender and refreeze in a covered container.

Use these recipes as beginning guidelines, but let your imagination roll and use any mixture of juices and fruits to create your own favorite sorbets.

Simple Syrup ➤

Simple syrup is the basis for many sorbets. You can make it up to two weeks ahead of time and keep it in the refrigerator until needed.

2 cups water
2 cups sugar

1. Warm the sugar and water in a medium saucepan over low heat, stirring frequently, until the sugar is completely dissolved. Cool and refrigerate in a tightly covered jar.

Makes 3 cups

Orange Sunshine Sorbet ➤

12 ounces (1^1/$_2$ cups) orange juice
^{1}/$_2$ cup Simple Syrup (page 176)
1 tablespoon lemon juice
1 tablespoon plus 1 teaspoon chopped candied orange peel

1. Mix all of the ingredients in a bowl and prechill in the freezer to a runny slush, about 1 hour. Freeze according to ice-cream maker directions.

For 2 servings
each serving contains

Calories	241	Fat	<1g
Protein	2g	Cholesterol	0mg
Carbohydrates	60g	Sodium	5mg

For 3 servings
each serving contains

Calories	161	Fat	<1g
Protein	1g	Cholesterol	0mg
Carbohydrates	40g	Sodium	4mg

Grapefruit Zing ➤

16 ounces sweetened pink grapefruit juice
^{1}/$_2$ cup Simple Syrup
^{1}/$_3$ cup sliced frozen strawberries in syrup

1. Mix all the ingredients together and prechill in the freezer to a runny slush, about 1 hour. Freeze according to ice-cream maker directions.

2. If not using an ice-cream maker, add strawberries after puréeing the frozen mixture in a blender.

For 2 servings
each serving contains

Calories	282	Fat	<1g
Protein	2g	Cholesterol	0mg
Carbohydrates	72g	Sodium	8mg

For 3 servings
each serving contains

Calories	188	Fat	<1g
Protein	1g	Cholesterol	0mg
Carbohydrates	48g	Sodium	5mg

Pumpkin Pump ➤

Halloween is our favorite holiday, but you can enjoy pumpkin all year round. It's high in beta-carotene and tastes great. This recipe takes an hour from start to finish, but preparation time is minimal. The servings are large and make a great snack as well as a tasty dessert after a light meal.

14¹/₂ ounces pumpkin purée
¹/₄ cup honey
1 tablespoon molasses
¹/₈ teaspoon powdered cloves
1¹/₂ teaspoons cinnamon
³/₄ teaspoon ginger
¹/₂ teaspoon salt
2 whole eggs
6 ounces (¹/₂ can) evaporated skim milk
Nonstick cooking spray

1. Preheat the oven to 450°F. Mix all of the ingredients (except cooking spray) in the order listed.

2. Lightly coat a small, oven-safe casserole dish with nonstick cooking spray. Pour the mixture into the casserole dish and bake 10 minutes at 450°F, then 40 minutes at 350°F, or until set.

For 2 servings
each serving contains

Calories	362	Fat	6g
Protein	16g	Cholesterol	216mg
Carbohydrates	68g	Sodium	726mg

For 3 servings
each serving contains

Calories	242	Fat	4g
Protein	11g	Cholesterol	144mg
Carbohydrates	45g	Sodium	483mg

Sweet 'n' Easy Compote ➤

There is practically no comparison to the fine combination of sweetness and nutrition found in dried fruit. When cooked into this compote, mixed dried fruit becomes a quick and easy dessert to enjoy yourself or to serve to friends with a dollop of honeyed yogurt. Use it as a great sweet-tooth satisfier. When made with prunes and apricots, this dish is high in iron, chromium, and potassium.

6 ounces mixed dried fruit (prunes, apricots, peaches, pears, apples, etc.)
1 thin slice fresh lemon
8 ounces cold water
2¹/₂ ounces plain low-fat yogurt
1 teaspoon honey
¹/₈ teaspoon vanilla

1. Place the dried fruit, lemon slice, and water in a medium-size saucepan and cover. Bring water to a boil.

2. Remove from heat and let sit, covered, for 10 minutes. Remove the lemon slice. Divide compote among serving dishes.

3. Mix the yogurt, honey, and vanilla together. Serve over warm or cold compote.

For 2 servings
each serving contains

Calories	244	Fat	1g
Protein	4g	Cholesterol	2.3mg
Carbohydrates	61g	Sodium	36mg

For 3 servings
each serving contains

Calories	163	Fat	<1g
Protein	3g	Cholesterol	1.5mg
Carbohydrates	40g	Sodium	24mg

Poached Pears ➤

You can bake an apple, but here we poach our pear. This high-carbohydrate, high-fiber fruit is made even better when surrounded by raspberry and chocolate sauces. An elegant way to end a meal.

2 fresh pears, peeled
Juice of **1** lemon
¹/4 cup water
1 tablespoon unsweetened cocoa powder
2 tablespoons granulated cane sugar
1 tablespoon water
1 teaspoon unsalted butter (optional)
1 teaspoon vanilla
2 tablespoons raspberry all-fruit spread
1 tablespoon boiling water

1. Place the pears in a shallow, microwave-safe dish so that they are standing upright. Pour the lemon juice over the pears. Add ¹/4 cup water to the bottom of the dish and microwave the pears on high for 5 minutes, or until soft.

2. Meanwhile, combine the cocoa powder, sugar, and 1 tablespoon water and stir until blended. Microwave the chocolate mixture on high for 1 minute, until it bubbles. Stir in the butter and vanilla until they are blended.

3. Combine the raspberry spread and 1 tablespoon boiling water and mix until smooth. Place raspberry sauce on each plate. Spread it out to coat the center of the plate. Place a pear on the plate and pour the chocolate sauce over the pear. Serve immediately, or chill the pears and add the sauces just before serving.

For 2 servings
each serving contains

Calories	246	Fat	3g
Protein	1g	Cholesterol	5mg
Carbohydrates	60g	Sodium	4mg

Banana Cream Pie ➤

Dessert can be nutritious. This is a great way to get in some calcium and potassium and still satisfy your sweet tooth. Reduce the fat even further by substituting skim milk for 2% milk.

1 ¹/₂ ounces fat-free graham crackers
1 tablespoon unsalted butter, melted
2 tablespoons water
1 banana, sliced
¹/₂ of a 3.4-ounce package instant vanilla or banana pudding
1 cup cold 2% milk

1. Place the graham crackers in a blender and crumb them.
   Combine the melted butter, water, and crumbs and pat down into a 4-inch pie plate or use a 1 pint casserole pan.

2. Place the sliced banana in the pie plate.

3. Beat the pudding and milk together for 2 minutes, or until well blended. Pour the pudding over the banana and refrigerate until set, about 2 hours.

For 2 servings
each serving contains

Calories	328	Fat	8g
Protein	6g	Cholesterol	24mg
Carbohydrates	60g	Sodium	480mg

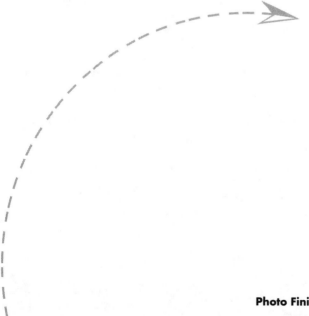

Strawberry Dream Cake ➤

This chocolate whipped-cream dessert is a dream come true. It is low in calories and fat to prevent nightmares.

1 tablespoon unsweetened cocoa powder
2 tablespoons granulated cane sugar
2 teaspoons water
1 teaspoon unsalted butter (optional)
1 teaspoon vanilla
2 slices fat-free pound cake, about 3 ounces total
6 large, fresh strawberries, sliced
2 tablespoons whipped cream

1. Combine the cocoa powder, sugar, and water and stir until blended. Microwave the chocolate mixture on high for 1 minute, until it bubbles. Stir in the butter and vanilla until they are blended.

2. Place a slice of pound cake on each plate. Cover with strawberries. Pour the chocolate over the strawberries and garnish with whipped cream.

For 2 servings
each serving contains

Calories	214	Fat	3g
Protein	4g	Cholesterol	7mg
Carbohydrates	44g	Sodium	155mg

Tiramisù ➤

This trendy, decadent Italian confection can now be part of your high-performance diet. Our friends in Italy told us that tiramisù means "wake me up," and the espresso certainly will. You can lower the fat in this dessert by using fat-free ricotta. Note that this makes 6 servings.

3 slices fat-free pound cake (approximately 4.5 ounces total)

¹/₃ cup brewed espresso or strong coffee

¹/₂ cup marsala wine (do not use cooking wine; it has salt added)

7 ounces part-skim-milk ricotta cheese

¹/₂ cup sugar

3.9-ounce box powdered custard mix (we use Jell-O brand)

1³/₄ cups skim milk

1 egg yolk, beaten

2 teaspoons unsweetened cocoa

1. Place the pound cake in the bottom of a 6-inch springform pan. Mix the espresso and ¹/₄ cup of the marsala and pour over the cake evenly to soak it.

2. Beat the ricotta and sugar together until creamy. Spoon on top of the cake in a smooth layer.

3. Combine the custard mix, skim milk, egg yolk, and remaining ¹/₄ cup marsala in a small pot. Heat on medium-low, stirring continuously, until the custard comes to a boil, about 5 minutes. Allow the custard to cool.

4. Pour the custard over the ricotta cheese and sprinkle with the cocoa. Refrigerate for at least 2 hours.

For 6 servings
each serving contains

Calories	245	Fat	4g
Protein	9g	Cholesterol	47mg
Carbohydrates	41g	Sodium	249mg

Cheesecake ➤

They said a low-fat, high-carbohydrate cheesecake couldn't be done. "They" are wrong. Our version is light and creamy, almost a cheesecake soufflé. Note that this recipe makes 4 servings.

2 tablespoons flour

2 tablespoons sugar

8 ounces Yogurt Cheese (page 53) made with low-fat lemon or vanilla yogurt

¹/₂ cup sugar

1 tablespoon maple syrup

1 egg

1 egg white

1. Combine the flour and 2 tablespoons sugar. Place 1 tablespoon of the mixture into each of 4 aluminum-foil cupcake-tin liners.

2. Combine the yogurt cheese, ¹/₂ cup sugar, maple syrup, whole egg, and egg white. Beat until smooth. Pour into the cupcake-tin liners and bake at 350° F for 30 minutes, or until firm. Refrigerate until chilled, then enjoy.

For 4 servings
each serving contains

Calories	293	Fat	2g
Protein	5g	Cholesterol	56mg
Carbohydrates	65g	Sodium	68mg

Peach Cobbler ➤

We aren't sure how shoemakers inspired this dish, but we're glad they did. Peaches are an excellent source of vitamin A, so enjoy! Note that this recipe makes 4 servings.

29-ounce can sliced peaches in natural juice (use all the juice), or use 3 fresh peaches plus ¹/₂ cup any fruit juice (we use orange)

¹/₄ cup raisins

1 teaspoon almond extract

2 tablespoons brown sugar

1 teaspoon nutmeg

¹/₂ cup whole-wheat flour

¹/₂ teaspoon baking powder

2 tablespoons sugar

¹/₄ cup skim milk

1 egg, beaten

1 teaspoon vegetable oil

1. Put the peaches and juice in an oven-safe baking dish. Add the raisins and sprinkle with the almond extract, brown sugar, and nutmeg. Place in the oven at 450°F until the juice begins to bubble, about 30 minutes.

2. Meanwhile, combine the flour, baking powder, and sugar. Pour in the milk, egg, and oil and mix until all the flour is blended in. Spoon the batter over the bubbling fruit and bake until the batter sets, about 15 minutes.

For 4 servings
each serving contains

Calories	231	Fat	3g
Protein	5g	Cholesterol	53mg
Carbohydrates	49g	Sodium	97mg

Bananas Jeffrey ➤

This wonderful dessert will satiate your sweet tooth and fill your body with calcium and potassium at the same time. It can be served without crêpes, like the classic dish Bananas Foster, or as a crêpe filling for a dessert with more eye appeal.

¹/₂ cup sugar

¹/₈ teaspoon cinnamon

2 tablespoons water

1 tablespoon brandy

1 teaspoon unsalted butter

2 ripe bananas, sliced

1 cup vanilla frozen yogurt (we used a brand that has 10% of its calories from fat)

2 crêpes, if desired (3 for 3 servings; see page 188)

1. Mix the sugar, cinnamon, water, brandy, and butter in a nonstick skillet. Heat over medium until thoroughly melted. The mixture should not be grainy.

2. Add the bananas and coat them with the syrup. Serve immediately over frozen yogurt.

3. To serve as crêpes, place some banana and some syrup in the crêpes while still hot, roll the crêpes, and serve topped with a scoop of vanilla frozen yogurt and a bit more syrup and banana. If the banana filling cools, the rolled crêpes can be reheated in the microwave for 30 seconds on high prior to adding the frozen yogurt.

For 2 servings, with crêpes each serving contains

Calories	538	Fat	7g
Protein	8g	Cholesterol	79mg
Carbohydrates	112g	Sodium	100mg

For 3 servings, with crêpes each serving contains

Calories	388	Fat	6g
Protein	7g	Cholesterol	77mg
Carbohydrates	78g	Sodium	77mg

Apple Cheese Crêpe ➤

This rich dessert can double as a brunch. It has made New York dairy restaurants famous.

1 apple, peeled, cored, and diced
¹/₂ cup (3 ounces) dry-curd cottage cheese
2 teaspoons sugar
1 teaspoon cinnamon
¹/₄ cup raisins
1 egg, beaten
2 tablespoons nonfat sour cream
3 crêpes (see page 188)

1. Combine the apple, cottage cheese, sugar, cinnamon, raisins, and egg.

2. Place 2 tablespoons of the filling in each crêpe. Roll the crêpes and place in a microwave-safe dish.

3. Microwave on high for 4 minutes, or until the filling is hot and bubbly. (Or you can bake at 450°F, uncovered, for 20 minutes.)

4. Add a dollop of sour cream to each and serve immediately.

For 3 servings
each serving contains

Calories	210	Fat	5g
Protein	12g	Cholesterol	146mg
Carbohydrates	31g	Sodium	63mg

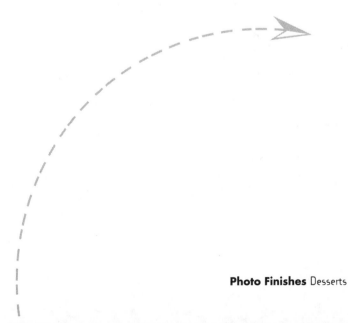

Crêpes ➤

The French have the crêpe. The Russians have the blintz. In China a filled pancake is mu shu and in Mexico it is a tortilla. Whatever you call it and however you fill it, enjoy this worldwide treat.

$^1/_4$ cup flour
$^1/_2$ tablespoon sugar
Dash salt
1 egg, beaten
$^1/_4$ cup skim milk
$^3/_4$ teaspoon unsalted butter, melted

1. Combine the flour, sugar, salt, egg, milk, and butter. Mix thoroughly and allow to sit for 20 minutes.

2. Heat a nonstick frying pan on high for 30 seconds, then spray the frying pan with nonstick vegetable spray. Pour $^1/_3$ of the batter into the frying pan (mix before each pouring) to form a thin layer. Cook until firm, about 3 minutes, and then turn the crêpe over and cook the other side about 10 seconds. Remove from pan. Repeat until you have cooked all three crêpes.

Black Forest Cupcakes ➤

I've toured the Black Forest region of Germany and have yet to see the cupcake tree; therefore you have to make them. Try this easy microwave recipe. It makes 8, so freeze extra cake portions and garnish when needed. (KRFK)

1 tablespoon vegetable oil
$^1/_3$ cup 2% milk
1 egg
$^1/_2$ teaspoon vanilla
1$^1/_2$ cups (12 ounces) cherries packed in water, drained
$^1/_2$ cup flour
$^1/_2$ cup sugar
$^1/_2$ teaspoon baking soda
$^1/_8$ cup unsweetened cocoa
$^1/_2$ cup low-fat whipped topping (we use Redi-Wip Light)

1. Beat the oil, milk, egg, vanilla, and 1 cup cherries together. Set aside. Combine the flour, sugar, baking soda, and cocoa. Pour the dry ingredients into the liquid ingredients while mixing.

2. When all the ingredients are well blended, pour into 8 aluminum-foil cupcake-tin liners and bake at 350°F for 25 minutes. Or use a microwave-safe cupcake pan and paper liners and bake for 3 minutes on high, rotate the pan, and continue cooking for an additional 3 minutes. (If the cupcakes are not done, continue microwaving in 30-second increments, checking for doneness after each increment.) They are done when the tops have lost their wet, shiny appearance.

3. When the cupcakes are cool, form a small whipped-topping nest on the top of each cupcake. Spoon the remaining ¹/₂ cup cherries onto the whipped topping.

For 8 servings each serving contains	Calories	133	Fat	3g
	Protein	3g	Cholesterol	27mg
	Carbohydrates	24g	Sodium	60mg

Frozen Fruit Bars

Make these, and you can almost hear the music of the ice-cream truck on a hot summer day! A great calcium-potassium medley.

Banana Pineapple ➢

1 banana
20-ounce can pineapple in natural juice
4 paper cups
4 popsicle sticks (optional)

1. In a blender, blend the banana, pineapple, and pineapple juice on high for about 1 minute. Pour into 4 paper cups, place a popsicle stick in the center of each cup, and freeze for at least 3 hours. Peel off the paper cup when ready to eat. If these will be frozen for more than 1 day, cover the exposed surfaces with waxed paper to prevent freezer burn.

For 4 servings each serving contains	Calories	118	Fat	<1g
	Protein	<1g	Cholesterol	0mg
	Carbohydrates	29g	Sodium	2mg

Cherry Strawberry ➤

1-pound can cherries in natural juice or water
4 ounces fresh strawberries, hulled
¹/₃ cup sugar
4 paper cups
4 popsicle sticks (optional)

1. In a blender, blend the cherries, cherry juice or water from the can, strawberries, and sugar on high for about 1 minute. Pour into 4 paper cups, place a popsicle stick in the center of each cup, and freeze for at least 3 hours. Peel off the paper cup when ready to eat. If these will be frozen for more than 1 day, cover the exposed surfaces with waxed paper to prevent freezer burn.

For 4 servings
each serving contains

Calories	120	Fat	0g
Protein	1g	Cholesterol	0mg
Carbohydrates	29g	Sodium	9mg

Caramel Fondue ➤

This low-fat dessert can be part of a romantic evening or simply a casual snack. You can dip other low-fat items, too.

5 caramel candies (2 ounces)
2 tablespoons skim milk
2 apples, sliced in eighths
4 ladyfingers

1. Combine the candy and milk in a microwave-safe dish. Heat on medium in the microwave for 2 minutes. Stir every 30 seconds. After removing from the microwave, stir until smooth. If the caramel is not completely melted, return to the microwave for an additional 10 to 20 seconds.

2. Pour the caramel into a small dip bowl and arrange the apples and ladyfingers around it. Eat while warm.

For 2 servings
each serving contains

Calories	366	Fat	7g
Protein	6g	Cholesterol	140mg
Carbohydrates	74g	Sodium	165mg

11

unBEATable
BREAKFASTS
early risers

Each of these recipes is written for 2 servings. Just cut the recipe in half to make breakfast for one. These recipes are quick and easy and generally can serve as an entire meal in themselves.

Cheese Danish ➤

This recipe is great for those of you who still yearn for doughnuts in the morning. It will fill you full of carbohydrates, calcium, and iron, something doughnuts could never do.

4 slices raisin bread
¹/₂ cup (4 ounces) part-skim-milk ricotta cheese
1 teaspoon brown sugar
Dash cinnamon

1. Spread each slice of bread with 1 ounce of cheese. Combine brown sugar and cinnamon and sprinkle on top of the cheese.

2. Broil in toaster oven until sugar starts to bubble, about 2 minutes.

For 2 servings
each serving contains

Calories	225	Fat	6g
Protein	10g	Cholesterol	21mg
Carbohydrates	32g	Sodium	261mg

Melon Boat ➤

This early-morning riser is high in potassium and vitamin A, two very important high-performance nutrients. The wheat germ crunch will also boost your vitamin E quotient for the day.

1 cantaloupe, halved, with seeds removed
8 ounces 2% low-fat cottage cheese
1 tablespoon toasted honey-crunch wheat germ
Dash cinnamon

1. Stuff the cantaloupe with cottage cheese. Sprinkle with wheat germ and cinnamon and enjoy.

For 2 servings	Calories	213	Fat	3g
each serving contains	Protein	19g	Cholesterol	9mg
	Carbohydrates	29g	Sodium	483mg

Fresh Fruit Crunch ≻

This great starter is a smash at the nutrient counter. It comes in high in calcium, vitamin A, vitamin C, potassium, magnesium, and folic acid. It's also a very high-carbohydrate, low-fat meal.

¹/₂ cup (2 ounces) Grape-Nuts cereal
2 cups (16 ounces) low-fat vanilla yogurt
8 ounces fresh blueberries
8 ounces fresh sliced strawberries (approximately 5 berries, or ½ pint)

1. Combine all ingredients and enjoy. Any other fruit can be added or substituted. On the road, add Grape-Nuts just before eating to preserve the crunch.

For 2 servings	Calories	358	Fat	4g
each serving contains	Protein	15g	Cholesterol	11mg
	Carbohydrates	70g	Sodium	352mg

Banana Dip ≻

This is a fun breakfast that you can get involved with while you eat it—sort of like when you used to read the back of the box of cereal during breakfast when you were a kid. But better than cereal is this breakfast naturally high in protein, carbohydrate, chromium, iron, and vitamin E.

2 tablespoons peanut butter
1 tablespoon honey
2 tablespoons raisins
2 bananas
2 tablespoons toasted honey-crunch wheat germ

1. Mix together the peanut butter, honey, and raisins.

2. As you peel the bananas, spread them with the peanut butter mixture and dip them in the wheat germ.

For 2 servings
each serving contains

Calories	309	Fat	10g
Protein	8g	Cholesterol	0mg
Carbohydrates	55g	Sodium	80mg

Grilled Grapefruit ➤

This recipe isn't a meal in itself, but it's such a great morning wake-up that we had to include it. And grapefruit really isn't only for breakfast. This dish, high in vitamin C, goes well with lunch and dinner too.

1 grapefruit, halved
1 teaspoon brown sugar
Dash cinnamon

1. Rub brown sugar into the grapefruit. Sprinkle with cinnamon. Broil in oven or toaster oven for 2 to 3 minutes, until the sugar on top bubbles.

For 2 servings
each serving contains

Calories	47	Fat	<1g
Protein	<1g	Cholesterol	0mg
Carbohydrates	12g	Sodium	<1mg

Peach Melba ➤

This peachy breakfast drink is packed with vitamins A and C, calcium, and potassium. If you need to take breakfast in the car with you, this works well.

8 ounces sliced canned peaches in natural juice, drained
8 ounces low-fat raspberry yogurt
8 ounces (1 cup) orange juice

1. Combine the ingredients and mix in a blender until smooth, about 45 to 60 seconds. Enjoy.

For 2 servings
each serving contains

Calories	200	Fat	2g
Protein	6g	Cholesterol	5mg
Carbohydrates	42g	Sodium	71mg

Apple Oatmeal ➤

This great high-fiber breakfast tastes just like apple pie!

2 servings quick-cooking rolled oats, prepared according to package directions

8 ounces unsweetened applesauce

1 teaspoon brown sugar

Dash allspice, nutmeg, and cinnamon

1. Mix the applesauce, sugar, and spices into the cooked rolled oats and enjoy.

For 2 servings
each serving contains

Calories	217	Fat	3g
Protein	7g	Cholesterol	0mg
Carbohydrates	43g	Sodium	12mg

Garden Delight ➤

This is one of my favorite breakfasts. It's high in calcium, potassium, and vitamin A, and it holds together while I'm driving to an early-morning meeting. (SMK)

4 slices whole-grain bread

1 small tomato, sliced

¹/₂ large cucumber, pared and sliced

Dash low-sodium Italian seasoning

2 ounces (4 thin slices) part-skim-milk mozzarella cheese

1. Toast the bread lightly. Make 2 open-face sandwiches of tomato and cucumber. Sprinkle with Italian seasoning and cover with cheese. Broil in toaster oven until cheese melts and bubbles, about 3 minutes.

For 2 servings
each serving contains

Calories	206	Fat	6g
Protein	13g	Cholesterol	18mg
Carbohydrates	28g	Sodium	380mg

Fast 'n' Easy ➤

This is so easy even our two-year-old daughters can make it themselves. With a glass of milk this easy meal hits all the major food groups.

4 whole-grain frozen waffles
2 tablespoons peanut butter
2 bananas, sliced lengthwise

1. Toast waffles and spread with peanut butter. Top with banana slices and enjoy.

For 2 servings
each serving contains

Calories	371	Fat	12g
Protein	10g	Cholesterol	85mg
Carbohydrates	59g	Sodium	516mg

Desert Bloom ➤

Cottage cheese doesn't have to be boring anymore. This calcium-packed recipe blooms with flavor. It is in the breakfast chapter because that is when I usually eat it, but it also makes a great late-night snack. (SMK)

8 ounces 2% low-fat cottage cheese
1/4 onion, minced
1/2 large cucumber, pared and chopped
1 small tomato, chopped
1/4 teaspoon freshly ground black pepper

1. Mix all the ingredients together and enjoy.

For 2 servings
each serving contains

Calories	129	Fat	3g
Protein	17g	Cholesterol	9mg
Carbohydrates	10g	Sodium	466mg

➤ ➤ ➤ ➤ ➤ ➤ ➤ ➤ ➤ ➤ ➤ ➤ ➤ ➤ ➤

The **High Performance** Cookbook

MORE EARLY RISERS

These recipes are a little more involved and are great for mornings when you aren't rushing out the door with breakfast in hand.

Eggs with Artichokes ➤

This dish is a takeoff of Eggs Sardou, minus the fat. For the perfect brunch combo, serve this with the Zippy Tomato Surprise (page 204).

2 tablespoons low-fat mayonnaise
¹/₄ teaspoon prepared mustard
1 teaspoon lemon juice
Dash cayenne pepper
2 English muffins, toasted (3 for 3 servings)
2 large artichoke hearts canned in brine, drained (3 for 3 servings)
2 eggs, poached (3 for 3 servings)

1. Combine the mayonnaise, mustard, lemon juice, and cayenne pepper. Heat on low in the microwave for 1 minute.

2. Place an artichoke heart on each muffin. Place a poached egg on each artichoke heart. Pour the sauce over the artichokes. Top with the second muffin half.

For 2 servings
each serving contains

Calories	363	Fat	10g
Protein	17g	Cholesterol	212mg
Carbohydrates	52g	Sodium	646mg

For 3 servings
each serving contains

Calories	338	Fat	9g
Protein	16g	Cholesterol	212mg
Carbohydrates	49g	Sodium	572mg

Mexican Breakfast Tortillas ➤

This spicy breakfast is an excellent Sunday morning treat following a brisk jog.

1 potato, peeled
Nonstick vegetable spray
1 small onion, diced
1 teaspoon paprika
2 tortillas (3 for 3 servings)
3 eggs, beaten
1/4 cup salsa

1. Cook the potato in microwave oven for 5 minutes on high. Cut into 1/2-inch cubes and brown with the onion and paprika in a nonstick pan sprayed with vegetable spray. Cook until the onion is softened and the potato has begun to brown, about 10 minutes.

2. Place the tortillas in a plastic bag with a damp paper towel. Microwave on high for 1 minute. Add the eggs to the potato and onion and scramble over medium heat until cooked. Place the scrambled eggs in the tortillas, add salsa, and enjoy.

For 2 servings
each serving contains

Calories	263	Fat	9g
Protein	13g	Cholesterol	319mg
Carbohydrates	33g	Sodium	105mg

For 3 servings
each serving contains

Calories	197	Fat	6g
Protein	10g	Cholesterol	213mg
Carbohydrates	27g	Sodium	70mg

Pancakes ➤

Pancakes are an American favorite. This version, high in fiber, makes thick, stick-to-your-ribs pancakes. For thinner pancakes, increase the milk to 1 cup. If you like, make these in a bigger batch and freeze them for a quick microwave snack.

1 cup whole-wheat flour
1 teaspoon baking powder
2 tablespoons sugar
1/2 cup skim milk
1 egg, beaten
1 teaspoon vegetable oil

1. Combine the flour, baking powder, and sugar. Pour in the milk, egg, and oil and mix until flour is blended in.

2. Heat a nonstick pan on high for 1 minute. Lower the heat to medium-low. Pour the batter into the pan to form pancakes. When the tops of the pancakes begin to bubble, turn and cook for an additional minute.

3. Serve pancakes hot, or take them on the road as a snack.

For 2 servings
each serving contains

Calories	330	Fat	6g
Protein	13g	Cholesterol	107mg
Carbohydrates	59g	Sodium	240mg

For 3 servings
each serving contains

Calories	220	Fat	4g
Protein	9g	Cholesterol	72mg
Carbohydrates	39g	Sodium	160mg

French Toast ➤

This version has a fruity taste. Use a great fruit spread or fresh fruit to top off this meal.

1 egg, beaten
¹/₄ cup skim milk
¹/₄ cup orange juice
2 tablespoons sugar
1 teaspoon cinnamon
4 slices bread

1. Combine the egg, milk, juice, sugar, and cinnamon. Beat with a whisk until mixed. Place the bread in the egg mixture and allow the egg mixture to soak in and coat both sides of the bread.

2. Heat a nonstick frying pan on high for 1 minute. Lower the heat to medium and place the bread in the pan. Cook for 3 minutes, or until the egg is set and the bread has browned. Turn the slices over and continue cooking on the other side, for about 3 minutes. Serve hot.

For 2 servings
each serving contains

Calories	380	Fat	6g
Protein	13g	Cholesterol	110mg
Carbohydrates	68g	Sodium	555mg

For 3 servings
each serving contains

Calories	253	Fat	4g
Protein	9g	Cholesterol	73mg
Carbohydrates	45g	Sodium	370mg

12

Gold-Medal BEVERAGES Power Drinks and Beverages

Fuzzy Navel >

This great beverage is high in calcium, vitamin A, and potassium. We especially like it a few hours after a good run on a balmy summer day.

1/2 cup (4 ounces) canned sliced peaches in natural juice, drained
8 ounces low-fat peach yogurt
1/2 cup (4 ounces) orange juice
1/2 cup (4 ounces) ginger ale

1. Combine the peaches, yogurt, and juice in a blender and blend until smooth.

2. Pour 2 ounces ginger ale into each glass and add half the yogurt mixture to each. Watch it foam, and enjoy.

For 2 10-ounce servings each serving contains	Calories	178	Fat	1g
	Protein	6g	Cholesterol	5mg
	Carbohydrates	37g	Sodium	73mg

Spiced Apple Cider >

The fresh apple cider available from our local orchards makes this taste of fall a memorable treat.

3-inch square of cheesecloth, plus string; or cloth spice bag; or tea-ball
2-inch cinnamon stick
1/4 teaspoon whole cloves
2 cups apple cider
1/8 teaspoon ground nutmeg

1. Break the cinnamon stick in half and place it and the cloves in the cheese-cloth. Tie the cloth closed with string.

2. Pour the cider into a small saucepan, add the spice bag, and sprinkle with nutmeg. Heat on medium heat until cider is warm but not boiling. Stir occasionally. Remove the spice bag and enjoy.

For 2 8-ounce servings each serving contains	Calories	225	Fat	<1g
	Protein	<1g	Cholesterol	0mg
	Carbohydrates	55g	Sodium	33mg

Fluid-Replacer Sports Drink ➤

Many of my clients have found that they like the taste of this homemade sports drink better than any of the commercial brands. Put it in your water bottle and use it before, during, and after workouts as a regular fluid-replacement drink. You can make a double or triple recipe and keep it refrigerated in a sealed container for up to 1 week. Freeze it in your water bottle for a cold drink on a long hot ride. (SMK)

16 ounces prepared caffeine-free lemon tea
2 tablespoons sugar
Scant **1/8** teaspoon salt
2 ounces orange juice

1. Dissolve the sugar and salt in the hot tea. Cool.

2. Blend the tea and orange juice in a blender or shaker. Drink cold for best taste.

For 2 9-ounce servings each serving contains

Calories	60	Fat	<1g
Protein	<1g	Cholesterol	0mg
Carbohydrates	15g	Sodium	130mg

Iced Mocha ➤

This healthful version of the higher-fat coffeehouse original really passes muster.

16 ounces strong black coffee (we like to use French roast)
1 tablespoon sugar
1 cup (8 ounces) 1% low-fat chocolate milk
1/2 cup (4 ounces) 2% low-fat milk

1. Dissolve the sugar in the hot coffee. Cool.

2. In a blender or shaker, mix the rest of the ingredients. Serve over ice.

For 2 14-ounce servings each serving contains

Calories	137	Fat	2g
Protein	6g	Cholesterol	8mg
Carbohydrates	23g	Sodium	111mg

Energizer ➤

This is a great high-energy drink when you've missed a meal or when you are trying to add some high-powered calories to build muscle. It is well rounded in nutrients and will help you meet your high-performance nutritional needs.

2 packets or servings Carnation Instant Breakfast powder, any flavor
16 ounces skim milk
2 bananas
2 tablespoons peanut butter

1. Place all ingredients in a blender and blend until smooth.

For 2 10-ounce servings each serving contains

Calories	414	Fat	10g
Protein	17g	Cholesterol	4mg
Carbohydrates	70g	Sodium	304mg

Zippy Tomato Surprise ➤

This is a great nonalcoholic drink for party guests. It's also a great eye-opener for a personal Sunday brunch.

12 ounces (1¹/₂ cups) no-added-salt tomato juice
Juice of ¹/₂ lime
4 shakes Worcestershire sauce
4 shakes lemon pepper
4 shakes celery salt
1 teaspoon horseradish

1. Combine all the ingredients in a pitcher or shaker. Stir or shake vigorously and pour over tall glasses of ice.

For 2 6-ounce servings each serving contains

Calories	36	Fat	<1g
Protein	1g	Cholesterol	0mg
Carbohydrates	9g	Sodium	21mg

Orange Juice Float ➤

We find this a wonderfully refreshing drink. It is high in potassium and vitamin C. If you want to avoid the carbonation, simply use fruit juice only and eliminate the ginger ale. This is a great substitute for high-fat frozen summer treats. Experiment with other flavors of sherbet and juice.

2 scoops orange sherbet
1 cup (8 ounces) fresh orange juice
1 cup (8 ounces) cold ginger ale

1. Place the sherbet in tall glasses. Add the fruit juice and then the ginger ale. Stir and enjoy.

For 2 12-ounce servings each serving contains

Calories	366	Fat	4g
Protein	3g	Cholesterol	14mg
Carbohydrates	83g	Sodium	98mg

Juice Spritzer ➤

Prepare this at home, or bring the ingredients to the beach and make it there. You'll have all your friends wondering where you bought it. Be creative. The spritzer can be made with any juice you want.

1¹/₂ cups (12 ounces) fruit juice (cherry juice is really nice)
4 ounces ginger ale

1. Pour the juice and ginger ale over ice in a tall glass. Enjoy!

For 2 8-ounce servings each serving contains

Calories	116	Fat	<1g
Protein	<1g	Cholesterol	0mg
Carbohydrates	29g	Sodium	8mg

Index

spaghetti cakes, 168
tortellini in broth with artichokes, 80
with tofu, 82
with turkey tomato sauce, 64
with vegetables and salad
  dressing, 58
vermicelli, rice and, 72
Pâté, lentil, 95
Peach
  cobbler, 185
  fuzzy navel, 205
  Melba, 194
Peanut butter and bananas
  on waffles, 196
  with wheat germ, 193
Peanuts, trail mix with, 168
Pears, poached, 180
Pecans, sweet potatoes with, 68
Pepper(s)
  bell
    chicken with, 136
    rice with, 164
    salad, 41
  hot, salsa with, 52
Perch, oven-fried, 112
Pie
  banana cream, 181
  chicken pot, 138
Pineapple
  and banana bars, frozen, 189
  chicken with, 131
  grilled tofu with, 81
Pizza, whole wheat, 99
Polyunsaturated fats, 5, 6, 17
Popcorn, caramel, 172
Pork
  with dried cherries, 160
  food safety and, 28
  with hoisin sauce, 158
  with mustard, 161
Pot pie, chicken, 138
Potato(es)
  and egg tortillas, 198
  baked, yogurt-chive sauce
    with, 69
  "fries," 67
  salad, 51
    with beef, 47
  sweet, with pecans, 68
Pots, 20
Poultry
  fat-cutting measures for, 26

food safety and, 28, 29
see *also* Chicken; Turkey
Protein, 7–8
  amount of, in diet, 16
  sources of, 8
Pumpkin pudding, 178

Raisin
  -apricot sauce, 162
  cinnamon rolls, 171
Refrigerator, stocking of, 21–22
Rice
  brown
    acorn squash stuffed with, 89
    with peppers, 164
    vegetables with, 71
    vermicelli and, 72
  fried, 73
Roasting, 23
  definition of, 24–25
Rolls
  cinnamon raisin, 171
  vegetable cheese, 170
Rotini with vegetables and salad
  dressing, 58

Salad
  beef, 47
  bell pepper, 41
  chicken
    curried, 143
    mandarin, 142
  cucumber raita, 49
  fish, 118
  fruit and nut, 46
  mozzarella and tomato, 45
  mushroom, 42
  orange carrot, 44
  pasta, 50
  potato, 51
  red cabbage coleslaw, 43
  tofu vegetable "egg," 86
  vegetable tuna, 119
Salad dressing, 48
  honey-yogurt, 46
Salmon
  mint mango, 108
  simple, 107
Salsa, cilantro, 52
Sandwiches
  grilled steak, 156
  grilled tomato and mozzarella, 195

About the
Authors

Dr. Susan M. Kleiner, a Registered Dietitian, earned a B.A. in Biology from Hiram College and an M.S. and Ph.D. in Nutrition from Case Western Reserve University School of Medicine. Susan has been the nutrition consultant for the Cleveland Browns and the Cleveland Cavaliers, The Repertory Project Dance Company, other athletes, and industry. She is a national columnist and speaker on the subject of nutrition, sports, and fitness, and is a member of the Gatorade Sports Nutrition Speakers Network and a board member of the Gatorade Sports Science Institute. She is an advisory board member and regular columnist for *Men's Fitness* magazine, and writes regularly for *IDEA Today, Female Bodybuilding* magazine, and *The Physician and Sportsmedicine Journal.* Susan is now living, practicing, and enjoying the mountains in Seattle, Washington.

KarenRae Friedman-Kester, a Registered Dietitian, earned a B.S. in Interdisciplinary Studies of Sociological Nutrition from The American University, and an M.S. in Human Nutrition and Food Management from Ohio State University. She has lectured both nationally and internationally on high-technology nutrition. She has worked in all aspects of the nutrition industry including: National Nutrition Policy; Wellness Programs; for a Fortune 500 company as a manager and troubleshooter on food and nutrition issues; and as a consultant on mammalian nutrition at The Cleveland Zoo. Karen has catered professionally and her family and friends enjoy her culinary experiments.